Codependency

the recovery plan. Be co-dependent no more & defend yourself from narcissistic & emotional gaslighting abuse. Heal from love addiction & improve self-esteem for a healthy relationship

Dr. Stephanie Sharp

contained within this document, including, but not limited to, —
errors, omissions, or inaccuracies.

CO-DEPENDENCY

Introduction

It is often noticed that codependents are mostly attracted to codependents, and that is why they end up having unhealthy relationships. But with proper commitment and support, you can reverse the codependent symptoms. If you do not check your codependent behavior at the right time, it can easily affect your thinking abilities. Well, you should also not think of codependency as something you can get rid of overnight because it doesn't happen that way. You have to work yourself up to your goal. But once you take your first step towards recovery, you will start to see the world in a whole new light.

Codependency is a behavior that develops in a relationship where one of the individuals has a mental or drug problem and another individual is so attached to the other that they put their own lives "on hold" in order to defend, love and protect their partners actions no matter how negative of an impact it may have on others.

Not only will we discuss the meaning of this behavior, but we will also be exploring Codependency's many other factors surrounding it. These other factors will be discussed after you have a complete understanding of what

Codependency is and the history of it. But what does codependency really mean?

This concept comes from the field of addictions counseling. Very early on, psychologists and social workers realized that it was not enough to merely treat a substance problem by treating the person who happened to end up in rehab. Rather, when you look closely, you begin to understand that addiction is a problem that affects all the relationships in an addict's life. Even though the addict's friends or family or romantic interests don't themselves have a problem with the substance, their behavior is nevertheless warped and changed by the presence of addiction anyway.

While it feels great to do acts of kindness for others, the codependent individual does not really commit unselfish acts of kindness for others. Their seeming kindness is actually a compulsive way to get what they desire – namely validation and love. Often a codependent individual will attempt to do acts of kindness as an expression of their low self-esteem, and therefore they seek the praise of others in their acts. The only way to know whether you are truly being unselfishly kind is to ponder whether your actions stem from a state of healthy sense of self or from feelings of fear, guilt, and insecurity.

Once you have, a complete understanding of what Codependency is we will then discuss the many examples of what to look for and recognize characteristics of codependency in yourself or your relationship and how to fix it if you are. You will then finish the book by reading great advice so you will receive a deeper understanding of the behavior in your daily life.

Chapter 1. What is Codependency?

Codependency is a word that you may have heard before and assumed that you know what it means; however, it is a much more nuanced term than many realize and covers a wide array of traits, patterns, and outcomes that go beyond a simple definition. In this chapter we will seek to define codependency and understand what it essentially is, as well as what it is not.

A codependent person is one whose life revolves around someone else, just as an alcoholic's life revolves around the consumption of alcohol. This person is hyper-focused on others in a way that is extreme and detrimental to the ability to have a normal, healthy relationship with the proper boundaries and independence. A person exhibiting this tendency will be over-reactive to others while setting aside their own feelings and needs. Additionally, because of their fear they will compulsively try to control others and the outside situation in order to feel safe.

Codependency Occurs in Relationships

Life is relationship, and to be alive is to be in relationship with other beings – whether they be the earth, animals, or other people. Our relationships reflect the primary relationship, which is our relationship with ourselves. The relationships we have with others can bring us much pleasure and comfort, but they will reflect the primary relationship we have within ourselves. If we are inwardly whole and love ourselves unconditionally without guilt then our external relationships will reflect this. If however, we have not learned to love and honor ourselves then our external relationships will be dysfunctional. Codependency occurs when we are not sufficient within ourselves, and so we seek fulfillment and security in our external relationships.

Codependency is Dysfunctional

Codependency is inherently a dysfunctional way of relating to others. One learns dysfunctional habits and patterns due to experiences in their life, particularly their early life, which reinforce negative beliefs. These patterns and beliefs have an innately addictive and compulsive nature, which make them even harder to be aware of and to heal. However, it must be recognized that the source of these compulsive and addictive traits and dysfunctional behavior is a codependent personality.

What Codependency is NOT

The reason why many argue over definitions of codependency and even whether it actually exists is due to the fact that there is not a clear line between what is normal and healthy behavior in a relationship, and what is dysfunctional. There are many aspects of healthy relationships that include kindness, compassion, caregiving, and being interdependent. Just because one is going out of their way to help another, this does not mean they are being codependent. Rather true codependency is when a person is giving up their own independence and desires in order to please someone else in a compulsive or dysfunctional way.

It is not caregiving

It is natural for people to enjoy and feel good in taking care of others and seeing that their needs are met. Many people, especially women, are drawn to careers that are centered around caring for others such as nurses or primary school teachers. However, there is a distinction between caregiving and caretaking. Caregiving freely offers aid from a place of sufficiency and abundance, whereas caretaking is done by an individual who is acting out of a sense of deprivation and lack. While a caretaker often genuinely wishes to help another, they also are struggling with inner feelings of resentment and often aren't taking care of themselves meaning that they are unable to truly help another. A codependent person will often give too much of themselves until the point that it hurts. This ultimately does not truly help the other person or the one who is giving.

It is not interdependency

A healthy relationship is composed of two individuals who are sufficient on their own, and are able to come together in a relationship from this place of self-love and non-attachment. However, in a codependent relationship the two people are interdependent, this means that each partner depends on the other. This sets up a dynamic of mutual reliance on the other to fulfill their needs, which can never actually work. In this type of relationship both partners will inevitably resent the other for any number of reasons. There is a never-ending struggle for power and control with each person directly or indirectly trying to get the other person to meet their needs. Two trees that depend on the other in order to stand up will inevitably fall. In a healthy relationship each tree stands on its own while drawing support from the other without depending on them in a compulsive manner.

The Essence of Codependency – A Missing Self

The common thread running through all codependent individuals is the inability to be their full, natural self. This is highlighted by the fact that the motto of Co-Dependents Anonymous is, "To thine own self be true".

Due to feelings of shame and low self-esteem, codependent individuals find themselves extremely insecure, anxious and cannot find their own identity and validation within – but rather seek outside of themselves for validation and acceptance.

Often these individuals are extremely sensitive to criticism and have a deep fear of abandonment which causes them to cling tightly to others. This of course creates a self-fulfilling prophesy which only causes others to attempt to pull away and leads the codependent individual to hold on even tighter and more compulsively.

Many times, the cause of this missing self in the codependent person is childhood trauma and shame. This leads them to attempt to become acceptable to others in order to earn the ever-important validation and love that they did not receive at such a crucial young age. The psychoanalyst Karen Horney created the phrase the "tyranny of the should's" to refer to this pattern of the codependent individual to attempt to mold themselves into the person they think others want them to be.

Chapter 2. How People Become Co- Dependent?

As you must have already gathered until now, codependency is all about sacrificing the needs of your own and giving someone else more importance than yourself. Codependent people focus entirely on people around them and not on their own needs. Their life is unhealthy and unbalanced. But how does someone become codependent in the first place? According to research, nature develops mostly due to the pattern of childhood upbringing, and it is explained in detail in this chapter.

If you have already diagnosed your traits of codependency, it is very common for you to wonder where they came from. You might also be wondering why it is so difficult to come out of such a codependent relationship. Well, the answers to these questions usually vary from person to person. But, as already mentioned above, most of the reasons will point to the childhood of the person. This is because, in childhood years, humans are more impressionable. Life experiences or cognitive abilities are not present at that age, and so kids fail to realize which emotional attachments are healthy and which are not. They do not understand that what their parents are saying is not always right. Parents, thus, manipulate and lie to their child and fail to provide a healthy and secure attachment.

Link Between Codependency and Childhood Emotional Neglect

Do you feel disconnected and empty from within but yet cannot specify what exactly is wrong with you? Well, you should know that Childhood Emotional Neglect or CEN is something that should not be taken lightly. It is very powerful but often remains untreated. It is often found that even those who have been the victims of CEN labeled their childhood to be good because they failed to realize that something was wrong in it.

The person you are today has a lot to do with your upbringing. Your childhood is what shapes you. All the emotional and physical needs of a child are fulfilled by his/her parents. But when parents are not able to fulfill this task, a significant amount of damage is done, and this is often invisible. When a parent fails to respond or adequately validate the emotional needs of a child, that is when CEN happens. Now, this is something a person fails to notice even when they are adults because CEN is not about what happened. It is more about what did not happen. There are no scars or bruises but only void and confusion.

Here is an example of how an emotionally neglectful family looks like. If the child came back from school sad because he wasn't selected for the school football team and then wanted to speak to his mother, who then shooed him away, then the child has no one to talk to. And then to increase the grief, the grandpa might tell him not to cry because it is not expected from a boy. No one from the family helped the kid process his feelings, and thus he was not physically neglected but emotionally. In some cases, CEN occurs in addition to physical abuse, and these situations are common in those households where the parent is an addict or is mentally ill.

But you will find several children who are victims of CEN but didn't face any obvious dysfunction in their family. They were not belittled or abused. They had parents who wanted them to do well but lacked the skills necessary to build emotional contact. Such parents are unaware of the ways in which they can attend to their child's feelings. These children grow up and become adults, and they might show that they have gotten it all together, but in reality, they are alone, and they have a void. They cannot fit in, but at the same time, there is nothing visibly wrong on the outside.

The person that you are today is hugely formed by your feelings. So, when your feelings are not validated or noticed, you start feeling that you are no longer important to others. Growing up in an emotionally neglectful family makes the child think that feelings are an inconvenience and so they should not be entertained. So, they start developing this tendency of pushing their feelings away from a young age or shoving them to a corner by taking the help of drugs, alcohol, food, or sex. Your internal state of self will remain unacknowledged until and unless you take care of your emotional needs. You will start displaying needy or clingy behaviors and always seek others' attention because you will want to prove your worth. You will be overworked in an attempt to find perfectionism. But the solution to your problem does not lie with external validation because they can never fill the void within.

When you do not have enough emotional attachment, you will find it difficult in your life to understand others, for example, your own children or spouse. When children face CEN, they are constantly told that it is they who are to blame for the problem, or sometimes they are told that there is no problem at all. But all of this makes life confusing for the child because he/she can feel that something is wrong in their life. As a result of this, they gradually start making peace with the fact that they themselves are the problem and thus start thinking of themselves as inadequate, incapable, and stupid. This belief, in turn, leads to codependent relationships in adults.

What is the Effect of CEN or Childhood Emotional Neglect?

When children are subjected to CEN, they develop certain habits, or several things can happen, which are listed below:

You Develop Caretaking Habits

In the childhood years, when parents were neglecting and didn't cater to the needs of the child, it promotes the child to become the parent to their own selves. Thus, they start developing caretaking habits. This helps them to fill the gaps that no one helped them fill. But what helped then in their childhood years didn't prove to be of much help when they grew up and instead acted in the opposite manner. When a person grows up in a troubled environment, they get confused between love and pain. Love isn't supposed to be hurtful even if relationships meant conflicts and disappointment. But a codependent person has the inherent habit of neglecting their own needs and putting others in the first place. That is how they end up self-sacrificing. They think that love means they have to be the caretaker to the other person.

You Come to Realize That People Who Claim to Love You Can Also Hurt Your Feelings

Children who face CEN are used to an upbringing where their parents had abandoned them, lied to them, never cared for their feelings, and in some cases, might have even threatened them. Such emotionally neglectful parents don't think twice before taking advantage of your kindness. You become so used to these things that this is what the idea of a family becomes to you. Gradually when you grow up, you let everyone come into your life and hurt you. You let your friends and lover take advantage of your nature while you give them more priority over yourself.

You Become a People Pleaser

CEN promotes the person to always try and be in control, and they do this by keeping others happy and becoming a people pleaser. They do not disagree or speak up because of fear that the other person might leave them. They keep giving so much that there is nothing left for themselves. They spend all their energy and love on others, and thus, at the end of the day, they are so exhausted that they do not have anything left for themselves. They derive a strange emotional fulfillment by helping others, even if it means putting their own interests in danger. This also subsequently feeds their self-worth.

They are so much preoccupied with what others are feeling and thinking about then. They have this overdeveloped sense of responsibility that they think the mistakes of others are also a mess that they have to clean. Thus, when people who have faced CEN grow up to become codependents, they get stuck in relationships where they mostly exhaust themselves by giving away too much and do not get anything in return. But the beginning of people-pleasing is usually with parent-pleasing. In childhood, they develop this behavior in order to keep their parents happy or maintain closeness with them so that the parents give them some amount of attention.

You Cannot Form Healthy Boundaries

When children are brought up in a household where no one pays much attention to them, they are unable to learn how to set up healthy boundaries. So, they either set up boundaries that are fragile and all wrong, or they have too rigid boundaries. When people have weak boundaries, they feel alone and vulnerable. When they are in a close relationship with someone, they tend to lose their own selves. They start indulging in sexual relationships with strangers, get into physical relationships very easily, and do not know how to say 'no' and so end up saying 'yes' to practically everything in life. They reveal their inner self and privacies to people who they have met for literally a few minutes, and thus, they start trusting people all too easily. When boundaries are nonexistent or blurry, relationships can become messy and scary.

On the contrary, some people tend to have too rigid boundaries, and they consider it their arsenal for self-protection. They get into relationships with inflexible rules, and they have this tendency to get isolated in every place. They avoid intimacy at all costs because that makes them vulnerable. Sometimes trauma is also the reason behind rigid boundaries that are being carried on from childhood.

You Always Feel Guilty

As codependents who have faced CEN, guilt is a constant companion. Such people set unrealistic expectations that are hard to fulfill, and thus, they are tormented when the expectations are not met. They are sensitive to all types of criticism that they turn to people-pleasing as a saving mechanism. Due to this guilt, people are unable to detach themselves from negative people, and this, in turn, adds to the problem of codependents. They have some set roles in life that they have accepted since their childhood years, and they think that it is impossible to break out of these roles. Practicing self- care also makes them guilty because they think that they are being selfish.

The very basis of guilt is based on the fact that you think you are doing something wrong even when you are doing it right. This is a tormenting situation. Codependents result from CEN when they constantly keep beating themselves up for mistakes they didn't make. The habit of feeling responsible for others' actions is also one of the reasons why codependents face so much guilt.

You Have Fear Tormenting You

Being constantly neglected since childhood instills a fear that carries on with you to your adulthood. Since CEN lowers your self-esteem, there are several types of fears that become deeply rooted in your mind, and some of them are that of abandonment, intimacy, rejection, power, criticism, and even failure. The number of fears in a person who is a victim of CEN is way more than any normal person, and these fears are also one of the reasons why they become codependent later on. The fear also leads to anxiety, which means they start apprehending about threats that might crop up in the future.

With anxiety comes powerlessness and unpredictability. Humans have been made to respond to every crisis situation with a fight or flee attitude. But you cannot do anything about some situations, and that is what leads to anxiety. That is also when people start projecting their fears and thoughts on others and end up sabotaging their own relationships. When a kid is brought up in a family that keeps on quarreling or bad-mouthing one another, the kid grows up to dread every family occasion because he/she fears that it will become a complete disappointment by turning into a battleground. So, they grow up to try and control everything so that they can prevent such situations from happing. That is how a codependent is born.

You Cannot Trust Anyone

People who have faced CEN have been treated badly and have been betrayed over and over again by their own loved ones. That is why they cannot trust anyone ever again when they become adults. On the other hand, trust is the cornerstone of any healthy relationship, but when that trust cannot be conveyed by one partner, the relationship is no longer healthy, and the partner becomes codependent. The partners are not able to discuss every aspect openly or be true about their feelings. Communication is often defensive, indirect, and reactive. There are so many misunderstandings and doubts that crop up just because you do not have enough trust among yourselves.

Keeping secrets, lying, and breaking promises worsens the situation even more. With CEN, people often try to predict the behaviors of people, and when something goes out of line, it raises doubt and mistrust. The lack of trust in relationships leads you to take matters into your own hands and babysit your partner, which is one of the core reasons for codependency.

You Are Depressed and in Despair

Depression and long-term exposure to despair are two of the very common reasons behind a person becoming codependent. These feelings result in hopelessness, and the person struggles with recovery too. There is always an unending feeling of crises in their life that they can't figure out. They feel lonely and abandoned by everyone in their life. Their needs are never met because they were neglected in their childhood and became a codependent individual, so now they give more priority to others.

They are in a situation where they feel as if every feeling has been taken away from them. When depression leads to codependency, the person enters into a cycle where they try to hide the depression with a busy schedule, dramatic relationships, or anything that involves an adrenalin rush. But when it all calms down, the depression starts to resurface, and the person again tries to bring some sort of drama into his/her life.

You Feel Resentment and Anger

With people breaking promises constantly and hurting your feelings since childhood, it is very natural to develop anger and resentment, and due to these feelings, people often become codependent and take control over every relationship in their life. Codependents who have also faced CEN often feel trapped, and relationships start seeming burdensome. They keep loving the people in their lives who cause all the sadness. They feel guilty to simply leave their loved ones.

All these unresolved issues that are mentioned above gets carried on to your adulthood and changes your relationship dynamics. You do not understand the distinction between healthy and unhealthy relationships and end up giving up on codependency. As a child, you had to undergo such neglectful behavior; you come up with ways of your own that help you to cope with your day to day life. Then you start thinking that your codependent traits are what helps you adapt to your current state in life. You start looking at your codependent traits in a compassionate light. If your parents were not able to cater to your needs, it does not mean that you are imperfect or flawed. You do not need to spend your entire life thinking that if you do not try your best to please others, they will not stay. You don't have to stay that scared little child forever. You need to break free from your cocoon and see the world around you.

Chapter 3. Signs of Codependency

One of the most difficult roadblocks in combatting codependency is denial. Oftentimes, one or both parties involved in a codependent relationship will have difficulty recognizing, and then admitting, the fact that the relationship has become unhealthy. Sometimes, an outside party or an intervention is required in order for codependents to recognize the issue. Moreover, there are instances in which codependents are fully aware of the unhealthiness in the relationship, but he or she is reluctant to outwardly acknowledge the issue or take action.

Luckily, there are ways in which we can identify codependency, which is the first step towards overcoming it and achieving a healthy relationship.

Firstly, it's important to separate codependency from interdependence. Within interdependence, individuals involved in a relationship are only dependent on one another to a degree. For instance, in a family environment, one parent might rely on the other spouse to help pay bills or carry out routines to help with the children. Likewise, the other spouse contributes in other, meaningful ways. This does not mean that they are codependent, or that they are relying on one another to establish a sense of self-worth; in reality, they are individualistic yet can still approach the responsibilities of a family in a shared, healthy manner.

Here's one way to determine whether or not you might be in a codependent relationship: ask yourself whether or not you are frequently second-guessing your behaviors and actions. Or, you might simply be experiencing an ever-present, high level of anxiety. Individuals in a codependent relationship are frequently judging themselves, reflecting on what they should have done or said differently.

In essence, one of the most common effects of living in a codependent relationship is low self-esteem. Oftentimes, low self-esteem isn't as easy to identify as one may think. Individuals who strive for perfectionism may actually be suffering from low self-esteem; likewise, they may outwardly appear to be confident, but it could be a façade. Inwardly, people who are experiencing low self- esteem may be ridden with guilt and shame.

Also, codependents are often people-pleasers. They feel compelled, and perhaps even responsible, for contributing to another's happiness. Typically, these individuals are fearful of saying "no" and may even experience anxiety when presented with a situation or invitation they'd prefer to decline. In many instances, people-pleasers will say "yes" to something that they may not have wanted to agree to, but felt compelled and will instead put another's desires and needs in front of their own.

Furthermore, codependents may have difficulty establishing boundaries. They often internalize others' issues, feelings, thoughts, or needs, and establish an unhealthy sense of responsibility for their partner's sense of wellbeing. Nonetheless, some codependents may become withdrawn and actively draw up their boundaries, making it difficult for others to become close to them. In other instances, codependents might vary the behaviors in which they establish boundaries; sometimes they'll let their walls down, whereas other times they might be completely withdrawn.

Caretaking is another common behavior found in codependent relationships. Oftentimes, the caretaker puts the other party in front of his or her own needs. The caretaker feels obligated to help the other individual, and might even experience feelings of rejection if the other refuses help. Moreover, the caretaker might become obsessed with the notion that he or she can "fix" the other person in the relationship, even if that individual isn't trying to overcome whatever obstacles he or she is suffering from.

Another behavior that might indicate codependency is overreaction. While most individuals do react to others' thoughts and feelings, codependents might feel threatened by adverse opinions. Instead of brushing off differing views, the codependent might absorb the sentiment and start to believer it; or, he or she might react oppositely and become extremely defensive. Either way, too strong a reaction to what should be an insignificant comment might be a sign of codependency.

Codependents also typically seek a strong sense of control. They might seek control over the other individual in the relationship, or they might seek extreme control over one aspect of their own lives. For example, codependents might become addicts in one way or another; sometimes, they'll even become workaholics to take control over one aspect of their lives in totality. Caretakers and people- pleasers might even use these behaviors in order to take the aspect of control to the extreme, using their influence over others to manipulate them.

Furthermore, codependents may try to control the other person in the relationship by restricting his or her actions. The codependent may try to give orders to his or her partner. Conversely, codependents sometimes won't let their partners participate in certain activities or behaviors that make them feel threatened.

While codependents often intrude on others' space, this can also become a physical phenomenon as well. Observe your behavior, or that of those around you: does it seem as if you're always spilling, tripping, or just generally accident-prone? Perhaps you're infringing on someone else's personal space, or vice versa. Establishing personal boundaries, both physically and emotionally, is essential to having a healthy relationship.

In many instances, codependents rely on dysfunctional means of communication. They may not be able to present their thoughts or feelings in a healthy, clear manner. Moreover, a codependent may have difficulty determining what he or she is thinking in the first place. If you notice this behavior pattern in yourself, it might be an indication that something is wrong in your relationship. Or, if you notice that you're unwilling or afraid to be honest with your partner, this could be a sign of dysfunctional communication. For example, if your partner asks your opinion on something and you're afraid to be truthful, it could mean that the communication has become dishonest, which is most likely a result of the other party's manipulation.

This is often referred to as the "doormat" side of codependents. The codependent becomes literally unable to determine how he or she actually feels about a given subject, because he or she is so used to simply agreeing with others to appease them. Nonetheless, it's important to establish your own opinions and formulate thoughts on based on how you feel. Codependents become chameleons, as their views begin to blend in with everyone else's.

In addition, at least one codependent (or both) in a relationship is usually given very few opportunities to get a word in, especially during arguments. One person may exhibit cues indicating that he or she is impatient, and simply waiting for his or her turn to speak instead of actually listening. That person has already determined what he or she is going to say, regardless of what your point is. Thus, the conversation will most likely become an unhealthy, one-sided argument in which one person's opinions or views will get squashed by the other's, instead of both parties trying to reach some level of understanding or compromise.

Finally, if you're concerned that you or someone you know could be involved in a codependent situation, assess the general emotions of the potential codependent: Are there signs of shame or rejection present? If you're suspecting codependency within your own relationship, have you sunken into a state of depression, resentment, or hopelessness? Usually, one party may develop a sense of failure: you might begin to feel as though no matter what you do, it's never enough to make the other party satisfied. Eventually, you could become numb and withdrawn.

You or your loved one may not exhibit all of the signs listed above, but chances are that if you've noticed at least some of these indicators frequently enough to become concerned, you may be part of a codependent relationship.

Chapter 4. Addictions and Addictive Relationships

Addiction is often a huge element to many codependent relationships. One partner often enables the other to continue in their addiction due to their love, support and desire to accept them for who they are. Although at first this may seem beautiful and positive, it is in fact very detrimental and destructive.

Addictions in relationships can manifest as the enabler (the non- addict who unconsciously or consciously enables their partner) thinking they are helping their other by paradoxically worsening their condition. This includes helping hide the addictions from others such as friends and family, covering for their partner and often deceiving others, making excuses and even going so far as providing them their addiction. This is in essence what creates the cycle of codependency.

As addiction impairs judgment, the ability to find solutions to real problems, and clouds mental clarity, in addition to leading to many negative displays such as verbal abuse, anger, overreaction, emotional blackmail and manipulation, deceit and distrust, it can be very hard for someone with an addiction to recognize that they actually need help.

When one takes the correct steps to allow their partner to seek help this often leads to an amplification of the problem. This is because the ego literally clings on to the thing that has given them pleasure for so long (even if it is clearly harmful and causes suffering) the moment it is trying to be taken away from them. A person's whole identity can become linked to an addiction and unfortunately the ego is a very strong aspect of self. The ego makes up half of an individual's psyche (the other half is the unconscious mind).

As the ego is only one aspect of self this 'clinging' and unhealthy attachment to a thing, substance or habit can therefore have some seriously detrimental effects. All other aspects of the self suffer, both on an individual level (mental well-being, emotional wellbeing, physical wellbeing, spiritual wellbeing) and in relationships and life.

Furthermore, when someone you love is spiraling out of control and showing irrational, detrimental and self or other harming tendencies, it can be very easy to turn towards codependent behavior in order to fight it. This in itself traps one in the vicious circle in an attempt to take control of the relationship. The non-addictive person therefore unconsciously creates a karmic bond which can be very hard to come out of.

There are many things one can do to start to heal either themselves from addiction or to recover from an unhealthy relationship with a loved one with an addiction. These include:

Learning healthy boundaries

Not taking things personally

Developing a greater sense of independence

Remaining positive and letting go of negative thinking

Counseling

Practicing self-care

Peer support

Self-hypnosis, cognitive reshaping, and neurolinguistics programming

Meditation, mindfulness and mantras

Sound therapy and nature

Herbal remedies and medicines

Often these are a lot easier expressed then acted upon and one usually only begins the journey to recovery from addiction when they are truly ready. If you have become entwined in a codependent relationship with someone else who is the addict, the best thing you can do is the advice above. Self-love and self-care is NOT selfish and it is essential you remember this. When you truly love yourself, you are loving another. We are all reflection of one another and harming yourself for someone else is not beneficial in any way, shape or form.

If you yourself however are suffering from an addiction, the best way to begin your journey to recovery is to take it slow and be patient with yourself. Balance determination and focus with compassion and patience, and incorporate all the exercises and techniques throughout this book into daily life. It is also important to know that seeking love and care from another is normal and natural, not something you should feel ashamed about. The moment you accept this, fully, is the moment you will naturally start to release some of your codependent tendencies. Remember: what you resist persists!

In terms of addictive relationships, it is usually (although not exclusively) women who have a tendency to become codependent in harmful codependency and therefore fall into a spiral of a detrimental addictive relationships.

Obsessive Jealousy

Obsessive jealousy and jealous tendencies frequently become a pattern in codependent relationships. The moment we start to become codependent on another for all our needs, our ego spirals out of control and goes into a fight or flight response. Our sense of survival and security become threatened because we give away too much of ourselves. Energetically, many people suffer from an overactive root chakra.

The root chakra is a very real portal of energy governing and being responsible for our grounding, our sense of security, protection and connection to the earth and physical world. Obsessive jealousy arises when this becomes over-active and excessive and we begin to function from a survival basis. Essentially, having an over- active root chakra is due to a disconnection from spirit. Codependency and spiritual awareness are intrinsically linked because, as explored in the material mindset and Western Society, being completely reliant and dependent on someone or something links with a strong sense of materialism, or in other words; being reliant on something in the material world.

This excess can be seen to have its roots in the ego. The ego is only one aspect of self and constructs only half of our psyche. In addition, we then have the unconscious mind, the self, the persona, the shadow, the anima and animus and many other parts to our whole self. Living, perceiving and experiencing only from ego therefore creates a major internal imbalance and keeps us stuck in cycles of pain, suffering and codependency. Our sense of independence is sacrificed and the self-confidence and autonomy we once possessed become lost in the ego's attempt to attach to another. This is the fundamental basis of obsessive jealousy.

So how does one get over this when the ego is so powerful? The key is to recognize that the ego is only one element to your whole nature and personality, and to take steps to connect to the other aspects of self. Dream work, meditation, personal interests and hobbies, spending time alone or with friends, connecting to your own sense of autonomy and independence, and establishing healthy boundaries within are all ways to assist in overcoming unhealthy and detrimental jealousy and obsessiveness.

Ways to overcome obsessive jealousy:

Meditate

Practice mindfulness

Acknowledge your partner's feelings

Start a gratitude journal

Begin a dream diary

Spend time alone

Connect to your inner nature and develop your own boundaries within

Treat yourself and be happy

Cultivate trust and self-esteem

Look to your past

Work on your shadow

Self-hypnosis

Have your own interests and hobbies

Cultivate self-love

Transition to inner beauty

Spend time in nature

Enhance communication

Get in tune with your sensuality

Express yourself

Let go of the need to control

Make a list of your partner's beautiful/positive qualities

Remind yourself of your greatness and unique gifts

Holistic therapies

Mindful movement exercises like yoga, tai chi or qi gong

Breathe and be Zen!

Whether you yourself are dealing with extreme jealous tendencies or it is your partner, this list can be used to help bring trust, intimacy and authentic connection back into your relationship.

Dealing with Manipulative Narcissists

Relationships with narcissists for those who naturally suffer from codependent tendencies can be an extremely painful experience. This is because of a fundamental difference in their nature. CD personalities naturally desire love, affection and human connection. They may have been raised in a loving family and the only negative aspect to them which creates their sense of codependency is from having excess love and attention as a child. Narcissists on the other hand are primarily selfish.

For the narcissist, life is all about serving their own self. In addition to a deeply rooted selfishness, they also manipulate and exploit others to get what they want. They lack remorse, morality and compassion and often genuinely don't see how their actions affect others. If they do see, they simply don't care.

Someone who has had too many bad experiences with narcissists can develop codependent tendencies and eventually become fully codependent with all its many negative manifestations. This is because it is natural for humans to want love and be cared for. It is part of our nature! However what is not natural is for so many people to be cold and display such high levels of narcissism. Over time this can have a deeply profound effect on an individual's psyche.

So when dealing with narcissists, one may not truly understand how someone can be so selfish and lack such compassion. Yet because this is all they are used to, they remain in a vicious cycle and thus further continue to attract narcissists as partners and lovers. It may initially appear like the cycle will never end as life has never shown differently. The best way to deal with a narcissist therefore is to begin healing and doing the inner work. Only then can one break the cycle of codependency with narcissistic characters for good and cultivate their own self-worth, self-esteem, and balanced independence within for future harmonious and loving relationships.

Explore all the various exercises, techniques and ways in which you can overcome codependency and self-heal.

Dealing with Toxic People

In addition to narcissists, there are many toxic personalities such as energy vampires, cynics, abusers, control freaks and compulsive liars. Let's have a look at these in more detail.

Energy vampires

Energy vampires literally drain your energy. They simply are out to take whether that be money, love, affection, resources, time or your wellbeing. Energy vampires feed on you and drain one or many aspects of your life. They can make you question your self-worth, self-esteem and even your own truth. Your sense of knowing can become diminished and, if you allow these toxic people to continue in their ways, your whole sense of self and independence can become lost. Once in a codependent and completely attached partnership with energy vampires, it can be very hard to come out of. The exercises and advice throughout this book however can help you do precisely this!

Energy vampires can either be active or passive. If active, they intentionally attempt to drain you of whatever you possess. This merges in with other toxic personalities such as abuse, control, and manipulation. If passive however they may not intentionally try and take your joy and happiness (or money and resources) away, but they are however constantly low, sad or pessimistic which they on some subconscious level wish for you to feel too.

They have no to little desire to lift themselves and heal and so they attempt to bring you down with them. They can bleed you emotionally, mentally, physically or spiritually dry.

Cynics

Cynics question you so you question yourself. They don't believe anything you say and furthermore actively choose not to see anything you say or do as real. They view life, your words, your actions and your truth with a shield and therefore can make you really question yourself. Motives, intentions, words, affections, stories and realities which may be completely real and accurate can start to be overcome with doubt if you allow cynics to enter and continue a codependency cycle with you.

These relationships can be very unhealthy as they specifically have a profound effect on your goals, hopes and dreams. Aspirations, personal ambitions and real plans and dreams can be sacrificed due to the cynic's ways. It is important therefore to recognize cynicism and develop healthy boundaries within so you can stay aligned and committed to what you know is true. Depending on the degree of cynicism in your partner sometimes you may be able to live and exist harmoniously together in a loving way, if humour and laughter can be an integral part of your relationship. However in a lot of cases, the cynic personality is too deeply destructive and the effect on yourself is too great.

Boundaries and staying true to yourself, your intentions, your beliefs and your talents are essential.

Abusers

Abusers are similar to narcissists as they can cause a lot of pain and suffering. They are however different in that -unlike narcissists who simply don't care, lack compassion and are inherently selfish -abusers often actively try and cause you pain. Being in a relationship with an abuser can be a very traumatic experience and wounds can often be carried forward and remain throughout the rest of life (if not healed). A lot of the characteristics explored in 'Communication: the Root of all Problem's' link closely to abuse in codependent relationships and it can be a vicious cycle. The best way to deal with abusers is to distance yourself as soon as possible and remind yourself of your own sense of self. Spend time with friends, spend time alone, immerse yourself in a project, hobby or creative pursuit and integrate holistic healing and spirituality into daily life. The latter two will help you see clearly how to deal with your abusive partner and keep you strong and centered within.

Often, a lot of what we attract is unconscious and therefore unconsciously manifested externally as a reflection of our inner worlds. Partners act as a reflection for ourselves and, sometimes, we can attract toxic energy into our lives to show us parts of ourselves we need to heal. If this is not the case and you simply have unfortunately become entwined with someone who reflects no similar qualities (in alignment with love, kindness, compassion, harmony, etc.) then the best way to recover is to distance yourself immediately and go on your own journey of self-healing. All of the exercises throughout these chapters will help with this.

Control freaks

Control freaks just love to control. They need to be in charge of you, what you do, how you fill your day, and even your thoughts and beliefs to some extent. They don't understand personal space or interests and boundaries are practically non-existent. Control freaks find it impossible to accept when someone disagrees and the need to be right can lead to some unhealthy and destructive interactions. Nagging, criticism, emotional blackmail and manipulation, deceit and an element of energy vampire energy are all common with these toxic people. They will control you to the point of breaking you down mentally, emotionally, physically and spiritually, at a core level.

This of course can lead to severe codependency. Sometimes laughter and keeping things light hearted can help but that can take a lot of energy and constant effort on your part. To overcome this type of codependent partnership, the most loving thing you can do for yourself is to leave.

Compulsive liars

Compulsive liars are extremely toxic and exhausting to be in a relationship with. They continuously make you question yourself as over time your intuition comes in to question due to the codependency cycle they have you trapped in. Initially you may be very strong and secure in your inner knowing yet the more they lie and you believe them, the more you fall into the codependency cycle. Once in it, the intuition and inner knowing you once felt becomes clouded due to your inner desire to want to believe them. Your need for them to be telling the truth and attaching to this reality inevitably means your intuition is sacrificed. This is when all sense of self disappears and you find yourself continuously believing their lies and not listening to your inner knowing. This leads not only to confusion within yourself but spills out to all other aspects of life.

Work, personal dreams and ambitions, unique talents, gifts and abilities, and your general confidence in life all can become affected when in a codependent relationship with a compulsive liar.

Over time, their lies can eventually become your truth, therefore it is essential to break the chains before you attach completely to their toxic personality. Like with narcissists and other toxic people, the best way to heal and move on from these people is to develop your own inner boundaries and focus on your own life. Exercises which work specifically with your intuition and third eye chakra (awareness, perception and higher knowing) would be extremely beneficial too.

Critics

These partners will judge you, and then judge some more. Regardless of what you do, what your intentions are, or how much positivity you create; it is never good enough. Criticism is a daily part of life and these relationships tend to be characterized by a constant yoyo effect. Each time you are happy, positive and on a high, or loving, caring and supportive, the critic seeks to bring you down. Unlike the abuser it is not a desire to cause pain and suffering. It is however more a desire to criticize and undermine you in some way. It is very difficult to remain positive and upbeat around a critic and they can often lead you to suppressing some of your beautiful qualities as a result. Kindness, empathy, love, affection, giving and generosity are all qualities which you will find yourself simply not wishing to exhibit over time. It is important therefore that you remain true to yourself and not allow a critic to 'burst your bubble.' The exercises throughout this book can help you do this!

It can be really hard to break the cycle with a toxic person, especially one you love and have developed a deep bond with. The main point to be aware of is that toxic people keep you trapped in their negative and destructive ways, and also make you feel guilty or shameful when you either try to leave or try to raise them up into a new light. They key is to recognize that you are your own person and do need to tolerate or appease their behaviors.

Recognizing the power of your mind and your own sovereignty are the best ways to deal with these toxic personalities. It also may be too easy to react and respond in the only way they know, for example if your partner only knows verbal abuse and insults or manipulation to get their way then you may begin to 'mirror' these negative qualities. Becoming the observer of your thoughts and learning to take things slow can be the best method to adopt here. Developing patience and becoming the observer of your thoughts (responses and reactions) allows you to not over- react or respond in a way which lowers your vibe or integrity, simultaneously preventing you from getting 'sucked in' to their ego games.

This is precisely what they are- games. The ego is not the true self and any action which seeks to harm, cause pain, belittle, control or dominate is not an action aligned to one's true self. Once you make the decision to stay connected to your true self, however, they will either have to rise with you and transcend their stories, or accept that a separation is in order.

Chapter 5. Codependency and Narcissism

The world of the narcissist is a complex and different one. It is different from how healthy and sane humans operate. That is why insight on how it feels to be a narcissist will help you learn how to relate. In understanding narcissism and narcissistic personality disorder, this chapter lays the foundation.

Understanding the Mind of a Narcissist

While many people have an idea of what a narcissist is, we are often clueless about what makes them this way. We often wonder what it feels like to be a narcissist? What makes them tick? What is responsible for the excess importance they attach to themselves?

As we strive to understand the concept of narcissistic personality disorder, it can help shed light on what goes on in their mind. With this, we know the thoughts responsible for their excessive self- importance. In understanding the mind of people with Narcissistic Personality Disorder, we should consider some of their characteristics. They display an exaggerated sense of importance with a need for constant admiration, making them appear entitled. Besides, their self-centeredness is alarming, with an excessive focus on themselves. This makes them dangerously envious with a constant need for reassurance. There is also a strong tendency for narcissists to compare themselves with others. It explains why a narcissist gets the urge to put others down or see themselves as more deserving.

This comparison is a vital tool in maintaining the narcissists exaggerated sense of importance. This comparison takes place in the mind, an offshoot of the critical inner voice. This inner voice is a destructive thought pattern coming from painful and disturbing experiences that form our opinion of ourselves, others, and the world around us. This cruel inner voice fuels the negative conversation going on in our head. For many, this mental dialogue can attack, insult, criticize, and is often self-destructive. It can be hostile and also self-soothing.

For a narcissist, however, what is that critical inner voice saying.

In people with NPD, their critical inner coach concentrates mainly on other people, and how to put them down. This is done to make themselves appear and ultimately feel better. If their boss happens to reward a co-worker, a person with this mindset may think: "He's an opportunist; I could do his job better." Or, they deserved that award more. If a narcissist is interested in dating someone, they are likely to think that being in that person's life would benefit them somehow.

Not only there are voices of comparison, but there is also the thought of wanting to be unique, an affinity for attention and admiration.

"You are clearly better. Do something to get their attention."

"What a fantastic idea, yours is the only worthwhile one."

"No one knows what is going on better than you."

"You deserve to be heard."

To a narcissist, this voice could be due to insecurity that is rooted deeply in his personality. It might also be as a result of an exaggerated sense of importance.

Whatever the case may be, why does a narcissist have to listen to these voices? Will they lose out if they ignore the voices?

Many narcissists have admitted that if they do not feel special, they are not okay. Narcissists operate on both sides of the spectrum. In other words, they are either great or they are nothing. They must be the best at what they do, and everyone must notice it, or it's pointless. This can be traced back to the root of the problem. A distortion in their foundation where they learned that just being themselves or ordinary is not accepted, they have to be the best.

An insight into the mind of a narcissist helps understand their action. Even though they appear strong and confident, deep down, they are weak and predictable. This is why a careful examination of a narcissist's behavior shows that their life follows a pattern, making them less enticing.

Watch out for the following patterns.

They Are Cunning and Have Mastered the Act of Earning People's Trust.

They always know just the right words to say, how to captivate people. Remember these people are masters of deception and they know how to seem caring and make you feel important, all in a bid to get close to you.

From a distance, a narcissist is playful, exciting, and lively. It is easy to fall in love with them as they are master seducers with a slew of romantic gestures to shower unsuspecting victims.

Once they have you, it's hard to back out. Your life and relationship will likely be subjected to abuse, trauma, and objectification until it ends. They won't show you their true colors until it's time because they know it will just turn you off. This is why so much effort goes into disguising their real personality.

As you proceed in the relationship, you find yourself reluctant to leave. You have a hard time believing your partner is the problem. This makes you always second guess the things you say or do, which would make anyone go crazy.

They Deceive Without Remorse

Honesty is not in the DNA of a narcissist. They can twist any event to a degree that better suits their selfish needs. Bear in mind that they do not think of their lies, as lies. For example, if they claim you are suffocating them in the relationship, they do not mind telling everyone you know that you are too clingy.

Putting others down means nothing to a narcissist. They target your self-esteem with their insults and abusive words so that your subconscious starts accepting it. With time, you start to look up to them for approval. People on the outside won't see it or them for who they are.

They Have a Deep Sense of Insecurity

Even though narcissists love manipulating and putting others down, true happiness is always far from their grasp. This is because anyone truly happy does not need to bring others down. They are a weak, helpless individual with the consciousness that they lack healthy human interaction.

They may not be able to express it, but they know they are broken. Deep down, this person sees the joy and satisfaction from everyday interactions and relationships elude them. Oh, what a lonely place to be.

Rather than looking inward for growth and self-development, they prefer to depend on others for their source of strength. This ultimately forms a pattern of terrible habits.

Types of Narcissism

More often than not, the word narcissist is commonly used these days. You hear it in the news headlines, day to day conversation, etc. Besides, many people hold the view that a narcissist is someone who thinks excessively of themselves such that others matter a little to them.

When you consider the way narcissism is used, you will think there is a specific pattern that all narcissism conforms. The reality is that narcissism occurs on a spectrum with healthy self-esteem on one end and NPD on the other. As a result, no two narcissists are rarely alike. They come in diverse personality with various modes of revealing their majesty. Besides, the way they affect self-esteem also differs.

Here are the most extreme types of narcissist you might encounter. They could be of any gender (even though, it is common to the male gender.)

Overt Narcissism

They are loud, have a desire to always be heard, in control, and never wrong. They are the most common. They have this feeling of knowing more and better than others. As a result, whether welcomed or not, they will voice their opinion and expect people to agree and go along with them. Things must always go their way and are not ashamed to say it.

They are bullies that believe in painting others bad to look like the good guy. They lash out at others and humiliate them without guilt. They are known to attack people by mocking and belittling them. They are gifted at coining words to downgrade their victims so they feel useless and worthless as humans.

The Covert Narcissist

On the other hand, the covert narcissist puts up a false image in a bid to deceive people. In other words, they will present themselves as kind, loving, and liberal but don't be fooled. They have mastered the art of manipulation to get what they want.

They are usually found in a position of authority such as politicians, teachers, leaders, etc. Since they are masters at deceiving people, they can pretend and put up any front to get what they want.

The Grandiose Narcissist

This is a type we are more familiar with. The grandiose narcissist considers himself as the most successful, more important than anyone else. He derives pleasure in blowing his trumpet and makes himself feel more relevant than necessary. They do this to make you jealous.

The grandiose narcissist feels his duty in the world is to accomplish great things. Truly, if you meet a serious and hardworking type, the achievement could be in sync with the ambitions. As a result, you have no choice but to admire them.

They love having the spotlight on them so any challenge to outshine them will be met with stern disapproval. They will increase their efforts to ensure you don't surpass them.

The Status Antagonist

These types of narcissists believe they are not worthy unless they receive the validations of others. With little or no sense of self, they strive intensely for power, money, and social status. This social status helps keep their self-confidence and intact. They use their achievement as a measuring stick to judge other people.

They are pretty smart in pursuing their goals and passions. As a result, they strive for headship positions: Chairman and Presidents. They only settle for second in command as a last resort.

The Narcissistic Winner

For the narcissistic winner, everything is competition. They have an extreme desire to compete in everything. This is not about competition in sports, academics, and career. It also involves day to day activities like friendship, spirituality, parenting, etc.

These are the type of people that get jealous when good things happen to their friends. Since life, in general, is a competition to them, they believe they are more qualified for the good things of life. They resort to belittling others achievement in a bid to make themselves feel better.

What Causes Narcissism?

We have passed narcissism as stemming from an inferiority complex and low self-esteem. This, most times, is a result of a discrepancy between the idealized self (standards set by others such as parents) and reality. This imbalance triggers a threatening situation which might be real or perceived, causing anxiety. As a result, they resort to defense mechanisms to try and keep the ego intact.

The narcissist employs denial in a bid to defend against the threat (even though that threat is not real) as well as fact distortion and various other techniques familiar to a person like this. Unfortunately, there is little to no research that has been able to pinpoint a definite cause of such a trait. The bright side, however, is that various studies have linked narcissism to genes and child development.

Genes

Narcissistic personality traits, like other disorders, are transferred through the genes due to an abnormality in the cell. As a result, the connection between the brain and behavior can become faulty. This explains why narcissist does not see anything wrong with their behavior, whereas a rational person would.

Environment

Oversensitive Temperament

Watch out for kids who like throwing tantrums to get what they want. They will cry, mope and sulk in a bid to get you to give in to their demands. These sorts of kids are prone to developing traits of narcissism. These kids believe they deserve special treatment which manifests even at an old age.

Too Much Admiration

When you shower a child with excess praise for a special attribute, it will create a distorted view of self. This is because kids relate this to self-importance. In time, they will expect appreciation for things they didn't deserve. The more apparent this admiration becomes, the more they accept that they are.

Excessive Criticism and Excessive Praise

When criticism is high, there is a likelihood of developing low self- esteem. If this continues, it can trigger specific traits of narcissism as a defense mechanism for self-preservation.

On the other hand, when praise and admiration are too much, the child can still develop traits of narcissism. This is because they grew up with the mentality that they are perfect hence should receive special treatment.

Overindulgence

This is not about disciplining your child for every wrongdoing. But if you give them a pass for every misbehavior, they will have no respect for boundaries. They will have no standards and believe they cannot be questioned for their behavior. These sort of children overly think of themselves as they can do whatever it is that pleases them, with no regard for the feelings of others.

Severe Emotional Abuse

Severely reprimanding a child harms their self-esteem. As they strive to learn who they are, they preserve themselves as they a means for survival. To make sense of what is happening to them, they accept that they are the victims in every case. This translates to a lowered sense of morals which robs them of empathy even when they abuse others.

Emulating Manipulative Behaviors from Parents

A kid will likely follow the parent's behavior rather than do what they are told. As a result of this, kids tend to learn the traits of narcissism from watching their parents. Be careful of how you treat wait staff around your children. Treating these people differently from how you treat your children sends the wrong message. Your kid will grow up and think it's okay to treat others like they are beneath them.

Who are the Targets of the Narcissist?

If you were abused by a narcissist, remember it is never your fault. As long as you are a human, you qualify as a potential victim of a narcissist. However, it is helpful to know the types of people that narcissists like targeting. This can help you identify any of these traits that may put you at risk and take steps to protect yourself.

Keep in mind that you do not only have to be weak and pitiful for a narcissist to target you. They enjoy going after strong willed people because of the challenge and joy of bringing a certain person down.

People That Struggle with Low Self-Esteem

Many things can cause someone to develop low self-esteem. It could be a devaluing experience, an abusive upbringing, any type of assault albeit physical or emotional and sexual violation, etc. These similar attributes make someone vulnerable to a narcissist. This is because the experiences over time have reconfigured the brain to accept that a person does not deserve affection, decent kindness or unconditional love. These types of people are alien to the concept of friendship and love.

Narcissist love preying on this particular set of people since they will bend their conscious power to them. This is what makes them an easy target for narcissistic abuse.

People Who Love Rescuing Others

If you have a passion for helping, preserving, curing, restoring, and defending others. You hate injustice and love to fight for a cause. You do not mind a little inconvenience to make things better for someone else, and cruelty to animals may set you off.

This is why you are drawn to the narcissist. Even though you realize you cannot cure that person you gravitate towards each other. You approach the interaction or relationship with the idea of making them feel a little better.

Empathy

Narcissists are easily drawn to empaths because only empaths can supply the steady flow of supply needed to keep them going. Since the narcissist lacks empathy, they are attracted to people that can provide the required amount. Empathic individuals are a great source of emotional fuel for the narcissist. This keeps them feeling good as well as relevant.

It is in an empath's nature to try to see another people's perspective on everything. This is an attribute that fuels the narcissist's behavior, which keeps the abuse going. To a narcissist, they know a simple apology is enough to excuse their wrongdoings. The empathic person, who is also always willing to understand their behavior, pardons their shortcomings. They know that no matter how much they misbehave; it is in the nature of the empath to forgive and let go.

Resilience

In a relationship, the ability to bounce back from abuse, fights, and most issues strengthens the partnership. This is why narcissists are attracted to resilient individuals as they quickly get over abuse. Over the years, resilient individuals have built their tolerance for pain. While this is a helpful attribute to keep one going through the storms of life, it can be used to keep them entangled in an abusive relationship.

Since it is in their nature not to give up easily, abuse is not enough to prompt them to pull the plug on the relationship. Despite detecting threats in their environments, they would rather ignore their instincts and fight for the relationship. To resilience people, they might even judge the love they invest in a relationship by the amount of ill- treatment they can put up with.

Highly Sentimental People

Sentimental people who love with all their heart are easy targets to a narcissist. A narcissist can easily employ excess flattery and praise to appeal to these people's needs. During the early stage of the relationship, a narcissist will idealize their victim in a bid to develop trust and appeal to their carving. They will strive to create abundant romantic memories that will soother their victim when the abuse starts.

Narcissists love toying with their victim's emotions. By mirroring their victim, they create a false soulmate effect which leaves their victim addicted to them. All they have to do to get a sentimental person is to manipulate their desire for true love. This is a natural desire peculiar to man but unfortunately, perverted by these unscrupulous beings.

Chapter 6. Types of Codependent Behavior

One of the biggest problems with codependent behavior is the fact that many people don't recognize the various forms that it can take. Just because the term "codependent" is a single term doesn't mean that it only has one face. Instead, it's a bit like ice cream. Even though ice cream is one type of food it comes in many, many flavors. The very same thing can be said about codependency. Despite it being one condition, it can come in many, many forms. Therefore, it is vital that you learn the different faces of codependent behavior so that you can recognize the signs that you are in a codependent relationship.

This chapter will discuss many of the different forms of codependent behavior so that you can recognize it in those around you as well as within yourself. The most common behaviors have been divided into four distinct categories, making it easier to follow and understand how these behaviors relate to one another. Most people will exhibit behaviors from one or two categories, some of which may be subtle in nature, while others may be more obvious and extreme. By understanding the different types of behaviors, it will be easier to recognize what type of codependent relationship you may be living in. This will help you to know which recovery path is right for you.

Abusive behaviors

The most extreme type of codependent behavior is abusive behavior. This is the category most people are already familiar with, and so it is the one that they readily associate to codependent relationships. Of the different types of abuses, physical abuse is one of the most extreme, and fortunately, one of the least common. More often than not the types of relationships affected by physical abuse are parent/child relationships and husband/wife relationships. It is a very rare occasion that any type of friendship suffers physical abuse, especially to the degree of what is needed to constitute a codependent relationship.

In the case of the parent/child relationship physical abuse often comes in the form of punishment. A parent will hit their child as a form of reprimand for an act that is considered wrong and undesirable. Needless to say, many people have physically punished their children from time to time, especially when the child does something dangerous that causes the parent to react in an emotional way. However, slapping a child's hand or even giving them a whack on the backside does not constitute physical abuse as such. Instead, physical abuse is when the parent beats their child relentlessly. Furthermore, the use of implements such as leather belts, wooden spoons or the like also points to abuse. You don't need to use a belt to get the point across, therefore such an act is extreme, indicating a deeper, more sinister root cause.

Beating a child is often done in order to gain control over their behavior, and this is where the codependent nature of the act comes into play. Any time a person tries to control the thoughts, feelings or actions of another person they are engaging in codependent behavior.

It is this need for control that induces people to physically abuse their spouse as well. Any time a person hits their spouse it is done as a means to subdue the other person, physically as well as emotionally and psychologically. Needless to say, a spouse doesn't require the same type of reprimand that a young child might need. Instead, any differences of opinion or mistakes can be sorted out through an adult conversation, in which both sides present their point of view. When one person beats the other in order to gain supremacy it is a clear sign of codependent behavior.

Abuse can come in many forms, not just the physical beatings that most people associate the term with. One such alternate form is emotional abuse. Any time a person acts in a way so as to make you feel guilty about something you said or did, they are demonstrating codependent behavior. The bottom line is that no one should ever strive to make a person feel guilty about anything. Even if the other person did something terribly wrong, to increase the guilt they feel for that act is nothing short of emotional abuse. In essence, emotional abuse is when a person causes another person to suffer from within. This can also take the form of inducing fear. Someone who engages in physical abuse may use the fear of a beating in order to gain control over a child or spouse. Therefore, any time a person tries to control the actions or mindset of another person by inducing negative emotions within them they are practicing codependent behavior.

Finally, there is the form of abuse that is psychological in nature. This is the most elaborate form as it requires a great deal of thought and planning to actually pull off. Therefore, even though psychological abuse may not be seen as being as harmful as physical abuse it is in fact just as devastating, and the person committing it is just as dangerous in nature. The most common form of psychological abuse is that of attacking a person's self-esteem. This can take the shape of attacking a person's looks, calling them fat, ugly, skinny or any other derogatory term that makes a person feel inferior to others. It can also take the shape of attacking a person's abilities, such as their intellect, their memory, or their ability to perform certain tasks. The overall goal is to undermine a person's self-esteem in order to gain and maintain control over them. Any time this happens it is a sure sign of codependent behavior.

Low self-esteem behaviors

Codependent behaviors can also come from the side of the victim of a codependent relationship. In these cases the behaviors are not abusive in nature, instead they are subservient in both form and purpose. After all, codependency is a two-way street, requiring both a taker and a giver. Therefore, it is just as common for givers to practice codependent behaviors in all of their relationships as it is for takers to do the same. Although the behaviors practiced by givers are safer and even more beneficial in appearance they are nonetheless just as dysfunctional and need to be fixed just as much as the behaviors demonstrated by takers.

More often than not the behaviors demonstrated by givers come in the form of low self-esteem behaviors. One such example is the need to please other people. Again, this behavior unto itself is not necessarily a bad thing. After all, any good friend will want to make sure their friends are happy and cared for. However, it is the extreme nature of the behavior that points to codependency. Wanting to please people from time to time is fine, but needing to please everybody all of the time is something else altogether. Yet, this is the nature of codependent behavior as demonstrated by givers. Any time you see someone endlessly trying to please everyone around them you know they are a giver, and thus they need help. The very same thing applies if you find yourself feeling the need to always please everyone around you all of the time.

This behavior can be taken to the next level in more extreme cases where the giver feels the need not just to please everyone, but to fix the problems in everyone else's lives. The compulsive need to fix other people's problems is a classic sign of codependent behavior on the part of the giver. Again, any good friend will want to offer advice when someone is having issues in life, however a codependent person will not only provide advice, they will want to step in and literally save the day. This need to fix other people's lives is dangerous, as it not only creates undue stress on the giver, but it also creates undue stress on those whose lives they are trying to fix. More often than not the giver will try to step in and take charge, feeling as though their efforts are normal and the outcome will justify the means. This can result in them being overbearing in nature, something that can mask the identity of a giver as givers are usually subservient and passive in nature. Yet it is this servile tendency that can cause extreme givers to exert themselves in a bold and commanding way, one that is overbearing and intrusive to those they are trying to help.

Sometimes the giver can demonstrate behavior that is more self- serving, and thus less obvious in terms of being codependent in nature. An example of this is the codependent behavior of overachieving. Many people have a competitive streak, and thus will strive to be the best in whatever it is they are doing. However, such actions are usually quite harmless, reflecting a good-hearted competitive spirit and nothing more. Givers take this to another level, striving to be the best at all costs. One reason is to compensate for the low self-esteem they suffer as the result of being abused by one or more takers in their life. Another reason, however, is to be the best so that they can better serve others and make everyone else happy. Either way, the efforts of a giver when it comes to being the best will be extreme, unceasing and potentially destructive, both to them as well as to everyone else involved. Their need to be the best will consume them, thereby clouding their judgment and causing them to behave unpredictably. If you or someone close to you is driven to be the best at all costs it probably points to codependent tendencies.

Denial behavior

The third type of codependent behavior is what is known as denial behaviors. This is where the individual cannot accept the reality of a situation, and thus rewrites reality to suit their needs. Such behavior can be demonstrated by both the giver and taker in a codependent relationship. The main difference between the two is that the taker rewrites reality in order to make themselves look better, whereas the giver rewrites reality in order to make others look better. In either case, the core behavior is that of denying what is real and replacing it with something that the individual finds more desirable.

Perhaps the most common of denial behaviors is that of denial itself. In the case of the taker this comes in the form of denying their responsibility anytime something goes wrong. Even when all the facts are blatantly obvious and point to the taker being solely responsible for a situation, they will deny that they are to blame in any way, shape or form. This denial can often be seen when a taker loses their job. Even if they are fired for poor performance, breaking policy or some other reason that is their fault alone they will deny the facts and place the blame on something else altogether. They may choose to blame the economy, stating that their company was downsizing but chose to fire them in order to avoid paying unemployment. Even worse, they may accept that their performance was to blame, but they will blame their home life for their poor performance, thus shifting blame from them to someone else, such as a spouse or parent. In any event, they will never allow blame to fall squarely on their shoulders. Instead, they will deny their role in anything that goes wrong, no matter how obvious that role may be.

Denial on the part of the giver takes another form altogether. In this case it is when the giver denies the harm that the taker is causing. This is often seen when a giver is physically abused by their spouse who is the taker in the codependent relationship. Rather than calling a spade a spade and accusing their spouse of abuse the giver will rewrite reality, accepting blame for the abuse they suffered. They may go as far as to say they caused the taker to hit them with their words or actions, even though they may not have said or done anything at all to warrant any kind of negative response, let alone physical violence. Needless to say, no action or spoken word ever deserves a violent response. However, givers will feed into the narrative that they are to blame for everything that goes wrong, and thus they will accept responsibility for the actions of those who abuse them in any way whatsoever. Anyone who denies the true nature of an abusive friend, relative or spouse is demonstrating classic denial codependent behavior.

Humor is another denial behavior, albeit an unexpected one. This is when a person uses humor to mask the pain and suffering, they are experiencing due to their codependent relationship. Obviously, this is a behavior demonstrated by the giver as opposed to the taker. After all, it is the giver who experiences the pain and suffering more so than the taker, therefore they are the ones who need to use humor to soothe their pain. Again, using humor to compensate for an unhappy situation is not dysfunctional behavior unto itself. What makes the use of humor dangerous is when it is used regularly to mask constant sorrow and pain. While many people can be jovial in nature, cracking jokes and laughing often, codependent people are those who seem to always be laughing, and they tend to be the ones who laugh the loudest. Furthermore, they are the ones who are always looking for reasons to laugh, such as telling jokes, pulling pranks or the like. The bottom line is that humor can be a drug of sorts, just like alcohol or pain killers, and a codependent person can become addicted to humor just as easily as they can to any other substance that provides relief from pain and suffering.

Numerous stories have come to light over the years regarding famous comedians living lives of tragedy and sorrow. Many people are shocked to discover that the comic personalities who are considered always happy and full of life are in fact suffering from severe depression, pain and emotional turmoil. It turns out that they used humor to medicate their suffering, and those who were the funniest were often the ones who were suffering the most. This is the nature of a codependent use of humor. When a person needs to be laughing all the time, never seeming to take anything seriously, they are probably demonstrating codependent denial behavior.

Finally, there is the denial behavior of unrealistic hopes. This is when a person denies realistic hopes and expectations, choosing instead to believe in something completely based in fantasy and imagination. In the case of the taker this behavior takes the form of the belief that all the things that are wrong in life will somehow resolve themselves without any effort on the part of the individual. Thus, rather than taking responsibility for their role in events the taker will rely on a savior riding in and rescuing them from a life beneath their true worth. Alternatively, a giver will live in the delusion that their situation will improve when the takers in their life realize the error of their ways and begin to live normal, healthy lives. Unfortunately, this is never likely to happen, yet rather than accepting the inevitability of their situation givers will hold out hope for the proverbial miracle that will rescue them from their life of suffering. In short, any time a person holds on to impossible dreams or fantasies, especially those that will fix the problems they have, they are demonstrating codependent denial behavior.

Victim behavior

The final type of codependent behavior to consider is what is referred to as victim behavior. This is where the individual, both taker and giver alike, view themselves as the victim in the relationship and act out accordingly. In both cases this behavior is intended to engender sympathy and support, providing the individual with the boost they need to feel better about themselves. However, victim behavior only ever enables both parties to be at their worst, thereby perpetuating a codependent relationship in which all parties suffer.

In the case of the taker, one of the most common types of victim behavior practiced is hypochondria. This has its roots in hospital settings where victims of injury or disease became addicted to the care and support provided by those around them and thus chose to be in a constant state of pain or sickness in order to continue receiving that care and support. However, hypochondriac behavior extends into every environment, including work, home and anywhere that a codependent relationship can exist. The bottom line is that the taker will create some issue that justifies their inability to care for themselves, while also creating the need to be cared for by another. It can come in the form of actual physical illness or suffering, or it can come in the form of a general inability to be self-sufficient. Ignorance, fear of failure, insecurity and the like can be used as an excuse to shirk responsibilities and acquire extra care and attention from the giver. In short, a taker will use anything to create sympathy, which is what they crave most of all.

Another way that a taker will use the victim mentality is to create a mindset that is wholly self-centered. This means that everything in life affects them personally, even if it has nothing to do with them at all. One explanation for this behavior is that it causes the giver to redirect their attention and sympathies from the actual situation to the taker instead. For example, if there is a tragic plane crash on the news, rather than allowing the giver to feel sympathy for the victims and their families the taker will put themselves in the spotlight. They may say it reminds them of an experience they were in, thus bringing up traumatic memories and feelings, or they may simply feign depression from the bad news in order to get the sole attention and sympathy of the giver. In any event, takers will turn the focal point of any situation into how it affects them personally, thereby getting the support and sympathy they crave.

Finally, there is the victim behavior known as martyr mentality. This behavior can be practiced by both taker and giver alike. In the case of the taker the individual creates a narrative in which they sacrifice everything for the happiness and wellbeing of others. Ironically, this is them projecting the actual role of the giver onto themselves. Even more ironic, the giver usually feeds in to this narrative, thanking the taker for their sacrifices even though such sacrifices usually don't have any basis in reality. For example, a taker may claim that by marrying their giver-spouse they gave up many other dreams that they would have pursued otherwise. Thus, they gave up potential happiness in order to provide a life for their spouse. Needless to say, such statements are improvable as alternate history can never be demonstrated. Unfortunately, takers use the inability to disprove such statements as a way to give them validity.

Givers use the martyr mentality to justify their subservient lifestyle and the sacrifices they really do make on an almost daily basis. Rather than accepting that they are in a wholly dysfunctional relationship they give meaning to their suffering by painting themselves as the proverbial martyr. Sometimes they see this as punishment for past sins or perceived wrongdoing, whereas other times they see it as their calling, one that they will be rewarded for in a future life or afterlife. In short, the martyr mentality allows the giver to justify their situation, providing it with meaning and purpose rather than recognizing it as a purely dysfunctional relationship in which they are being abused and taken advantage of. Unfortunately, by finding meaning in this way the giver further commits themselves to their role in the codependent relationship, thereby ensuring that it continues to live on day after day, week after week and year after year.

Chapter 7. Detaching from Codependent Influences

The number one rule of breaking free from a codependent relationship is to recognize that you can never change the other person. Only when you come to terms with this fact can you begin to take the measures necessary to liberate yourself from the influences and effects of a dysfunctional relationship. One such measure is to practice what is referred to as detachment. Simply put, detachment is the process of removing yourself from the codependent equation. This can be achieved by avoiding arguments, ending the role of being responsible for other peoples' happiness, or by stopping any other action that contributes to the codependent nature of the relationship. This chapter will discuss several methods for detaching from codependent influences, thereby providing you with the tools you need to begin to free yourself from the harm such influences can cause. Once you have read this chapter you will be able to begin your journey to liberating yourself from codependent relationships and creating the healthy and happy life you both desire and deserve.

Recognize you aren't responsible for other peoples' happiness

The first step toward achieving detachment is to change your way of thinking. This covers a wide range of areas, so it is something that cannot be done all at once. Instead, it is a process that must be achieved one step at a time. While there is no wrong place to start as such, perhaps the easiest and most important place to start changing your way of thinking is in regards to other people's happiness. The bottom line is that you aren't responsible for how other people feel, no matter what others might say. Only when you come to this realization can you begin to move on with your life in a healthy and meaningful way.

This change in mindset will take a while to develop, as your current mindset is probably the result of years of conditioning. Subsequently, it is important that you don't look for immediate results. Instead, treat this the way you would if you were trying to develop muscle strength or lose weight. You wouldn't expect to walk into the gym one or two times and come out looking like a body builder. Similarly, you wouldn't expect to eat a salad or two and miraculously drop ten or twenty pounds of extra weight. Instead, you recognize that any meaningful results will take time. Therefore, expect these results to take the same time and effort. This way you can commit to the long game, allowing yourself the time needed to make the progress you desire.

The easiest way to begin recognizing that you aren't responsible for other peoples' happiness is to simply stop taking responsibility for all of their choices. If the taker in your relationship relies on you making the right decisions in order for them to be happy start demanding that they begin to share in the decision making process. This doesn't have to be an all or nothing scenario, rather it can be a step by step process in which you slowly turn over the burden of responsibility to the other person for finding happiness in their life. You might start by forcing them to choose between a few options rather than making all the choices yourself. For example, if you are planning to go out on a date, instead of making every decision yourself come up with a few options you think might work and make the other person choose one. This is a perfect balance that allows both parties to make decisions together, rather than relying on one person to be fully in charge.

Needless to say, there may be times when the taker puts up a fuss and refuses to play along. This is a classic attempt to maintain the status quo on their part, so don't allow them to hinder your efforts. Instead, expect resistance at first, but realize that once you cross the initial hurdle things will begin to get easier. Like it or not, the taker will have to adapt to your gradual changes or else face the possibility of more extreme changes, such as losing you altogether. They will only recognize such a choice if you stick to your guns, so don't let them bully you out of making this positive change in your life.

Recognize you aren't responsible for other peoples' unhappiness

The next step toward detaching from codependent influences is to recognize that you aren't responsible for other peoples' unhappiness. Again, this is all about realizing that every person is ultimately responsible for how they feel, both happy and otherwise. Unfortunately, in the case of a codependent relationship you will be made to take the blame for when the taker is unhappy, no matter what the reason might be. Even if you aren't directly responsible for the action or situation that causes their unhappiness, the taker will still blame you for not protecting them more effectively from those things that brought them misery. Needless to say, this is about as unrealistic a mindset as you could imagine, one that usually creates a sense of hopelessness on the part of the giver. After all, you can't possibly protect a person from everything that might cause them to become unhappy, no matter how hard you try. Therefore, the mission is as impossible as it is hopeless.

In order to put this overwhelming hopelessness behind you once and for all you need to begin to change your perspective on things. Again, it is vital that you understand that no individual is responsible for someone else's happiness, sadness or any other state of mind. Therefore, don't feed in to the narrative that you are to blame when the taker in the relationship is angry, sad or depressed. Instead, take a step back and recognize the impact that the taker's choices had on their overall emotional wellbeing. The chances are you can trace their unhappiness to their past choices or behavior. Once you do this you realize that their unhappiness is the result of their own actions, not yours. After a while you will start to see a pattern, one that reveals the simple truth that the taker is solely responsible for their overall wellbeing. This will help you to change your perspective on things, thereby freeing you from the guilt for failing to protect others from being unhappy. The bottom line is that you didn't fail, therefore you are guilt free.

How you handle this change of perspective can be a bit tricky. The bottom line is you don't want to use this newfound information as fodder for arguments or conflict. This will only serve to make the relationship more volatile, thereby undermining your efforts to improve the situation. Therefore, the best thing is to simply not play the game of apologizing for how other people feel. After all, this is the essence of detachment. The goal isn't to change the other person, or to lead them to some sort of enlightenment. Instead, the goal is to remove yourself from the cycle of codependence, thereby allowing you to live a healthier and happier life. That said, by not feeding into the blame game you will achieve your goal, even if the taker in the relationship doesn't change their attitude.

Begin to make decisions for yourself

The basic lesson to be learned with regard to how a person feels is that it all comes down to the decisions the individual makes.

When a person makes good, positive choices then they are likely to be happy and content with their life. Alternatively, when they make bad, negative choices they will be unhappy and frustrated with their day- to-day existence. That said, now that you have freed yourself from the idea that you are responsible for how other people feel the next step toward detachment from codependent influences is to start making decisions for yourself. This not only allows you to break free from the cycle of codependency, it actually enables you to move forward with your life, creating a life of happiness, fulfillment and meaning. By making decisions for yourself you can start to shape your life in a way you never imagined possible!

You might find this process difficult to get used to at first. This is because you have probably spent most of your life feeling as though every decision you made had to be about everyone else and not about you. The chances are you never took the time to consider how you felt about the choices you had to make. Instead, you looked at the options you had to choose from and tried to decide which option would be more pleasing to the other people in your life. In a way, it's a bit like constantly Christmas shopping for other people. Every decision you made was an attempt to bring happiness to others, never to bring happiness to yourself. In order to move on with your life you need to begin to turn that thought process around and start making decisions for yourself rather than for other people. Only then can you truly be free of the controlling influences of a codependent relationship.

At first this process might sound like one that will be exciting and fun, as though you have reached the stage of your journey that rewards you for all the hard work you have put in. While this can be true the chances are this stage will be one of the most difficult for you to get through. The main reason for this is that making decision for yourself goes against every codependent influence that you have been put under. Your whole life has been spent in the service of others. Thus the idea of actually doing things for yourself will be very difficult to adapt to. One of the main obstacles you will encounter is that of feeling selfish. Since your life has so far been spent doing things for others the idea of doing things for yourself will seem strange and alien. You will feel self-conscious making a decision for the sole reason of bringing yourself happiness and pleasure. However, this is a vital hurdle to overcome, one that will prove a turning point on your road to a normal and healthy life.

Another challenge you will face will be that of feeling guilty for any decision you make for yourself. This can be especially true in the case of buying things that you want or need. In most codependent relationships the giver will go without such things as new shoes or other necessities since their wellbeing is seen as secondary to that of the taker. However, once you break free from that cycle you will begin to put your needs first. Again, initially you will probably feel guilty, telling yourself that you could have spent the money on something or someone else rather than the item you chose to buy. This is the codependent programming coming to surface, so it is vital that you don't give in to it and return things or avoid buying them in the first place. Instead, you must make firm decisions and stick to them, only then can you begin to reprogram your way of thinking and thus be free of codependent influences once and for all.

In some cases the opposite scenario may play out, the one in which you start buying anything and everything your heart desires. This can have equally negative consequences, especially when the bill arrives in the mail! Such binge shopping is understandable, however, since you have years of self-pampering to make up for. Fortunately, there is a simple trick that can help you to avoid binge shopping as well as any feelings of guilt that you might experience as mentioned before. This trick is to create a wish list. Simply write down all the things you want or need, regardless of price, size or importance. Write down everything you would buy if money were no object. Once you have created this list go back through it, one item at a time, and decide which items to keep and which items to remove. Start by keeping those items that you need to buy. This will ensure you purchase only those things you can justify, which will help to overcome or even prevent any feelings of guilt.

Another effective trick is to buy one thing at a time, spacing out the shopping experience in order to keep from feeling overwhelmed. You can choose to buy one thing a week, thereby curbing your spending as well as giving you something to look forward to. Once you have crossed off all the items on your need list you can create a list of the things you want. These can be purchased on an even more infrequent basis, such as once a month, thereby helping you to ease into the process of buying things for the sole purpose of bringing you pleasure. This same process holds true for any decision making paradigm. No matter what the decisions are the important thing is to start with your needs and then extend to your wants. This will enable you to develop the habit of choosing for yourself while maintaining some level of discipline that will keep you from losing control.

Become self-aware

When it comes to making decisions for yourself you might run into the common snag of not actually knowing what you want. This is something most victims of codependent relationships experience at first due to the fact that they never took the time to consider their feelings or desires before. Instead, they always considered the feelings and desires of others when making every decision or choice that they had to make. As a result, you may find it difficult to make choices for yourself since you may not actually know what things you like and what things you don't like. In order to overcome this obstacle you must become self-aware.

The idea of becoming self-aware might sound like some Zen ideal that requires hours of meditation or yoga to achieve. Fortunately, while meditation and yoga can help to achieve a deep level of self- awareness they aren't required for the level you need at this point. Rather than needing to figure out your place in the Universe, the self- awareness you are looking for right now is what your favorite color is, or what ice cream flavor you like best. As such, the path to this level of self-awareness can be a fun and exciting one, requiring more daring than discipline as in the case of meditation or yoga! The trick is to treat this as a time of self-discovery, one that allows you to meet yourself for the very first time.

Since most choices are subjective in nature there isn't really a right or wrong answer. Instead, it comes down to a matter of preference. This is especially true in the case of what your favorite color is or what your favorite ice cream is. At first you might feel anxious when trying to make decisions on such matters as you probably don't know the answers. However, rather than stressing out about it simply explore life, making one choice at a time and learning as much as you can along the way. For example, don't be afraid to try different flavors and colors until you find the ones that work for you. The choices you make in life should bring you joy, therefore find the things that make you happy and then start choosing them on a regular basis. If you make a choice that isn't happy don't feel as though you failed or made a mistake. Instead, recognize that choice isn't right for you and don't make it again.

Another type of self-awareness you will want to develop is that of being aware of your feelings. Anyone who has been victim of a codependent relationship will have had to suppress their emotions and feelings in order to focus on the feelings and needs of others.

Subsequently, you might not actually know how you feel at any given time. It is vital to develop the ability to know how you are feeling so that you can practice greater self-care in many of life's situations. Fortunately, developing this self-awareness is actually quite easy, requiring only a small amount of time and effort to achieve. The simple trick is to take a few moments during the day to ask yourself how you are feeling. At first you will want to choose a time where you are alone and uninterrupted, such as first thing in the morning or the last thing at night. Simply ask yourself how you feel and take the time to discover the answer.

You may struggle to answer the question at first since you are likely out of touch with your feelings. However, it is vital that you do answer the question, even if the answer seems a bit strange. For example, if you neither feel happy nor sad then simply state that you feel indifferent and leave that as your answer.

Alternatively, if you do feel something, even just a tingling sense of happiness, sadness, or some other emotion, then state that as your answer. You don't have to feel overwhelming emotions at every point of the day. You just have to recognize the emotions you have, large or small. The important thing is to not stress about it, instead understand that you will discover your feelings in time.

Once you have mastered the ability to determine your feelings in the safe space of your home you can start extending the practice into the other environments of your day-to-day life. While at work you can ask yourself how you feel at various points, thereby recognizing the impact different people or events have on your mindset. The important thing is to become self-aware so that you shift your attention from the thoughts and feelings of others to your own thoughts and feelings. Only then can you live your own life in a real and meaningful way, making the right choices for you and taking actions that serve to benefit you and bring you the happiness and satisfaction you truly deserve.

Accept the truth

The final step to achieving detachment from codependent influences is to accept the truth. In this case the truth is summed up in the word "detach" itself. Don't Even Think About Changing Him/ Her. The most important lesson to learn is that the other person in your relationship is probably beyond changing, thus any time and effort you spend trying to fix them will prove wasted. In fact, the more you try to fix the taker in a codependent relationship the worse things will usually get. Takers don't want to heal, they only want to keep taking. This goes back to the example of the sick person never recovering in a hospital. Such a person doesn't want to get healthy since getting healthy means having to take care of themselves and losing the support of the giver. Therefore they want to stay sick so that they can be cared for on a continual basis. Trying to fix them is ignoring the fundamental truth that they want to remain broken.

Furthermore, trying to fix other people is one of the main behaviors of a giver, making it a codependent tendency. If you want to detach from codependent influences you must eliminate any behaviors within your own life that would enable a codependent relationship, including the urge to fix other people. Therefore, rather than trying to fix the relationship and everyone involved the key is to fix yourself, thereby removing yourself from the equation and thus ending the cycle of codependency. Only by accepting this truth can you effectively let go of the codependent influences in your life and begin to move on, creating a life of freedom and happiness for yourself.

Chapter 8. The Habits of Codependent Individuals

Please people at their own expense

Codependents are people-pleasers, that is, they try their best to satisfy the needs and wants of everybody around them. They are always the first to respond to calls for help. The "hero" chromosome in them always pushes them to the front queue of helpers and saviors whenever one is needed. They have an intense need to provide help, and they feed it upon the problems of their friends and family members. Often though, they provide help and care at their own expense. They go the extra lengths even if it means getting burned to make themselves indispensable to anybody that might require help.

Discomfort with receiving attention or help from others

Unfortunately, codependents do have scruples with asking for and receiving help. They have been conditioned to keep their emotions and needs close to their chest while growing up and cannot bring themselves to show what they see as weakness. Therefore, they suffer in silence. They don't ask for help and would rather brave the waters on their own. When they receive help such as cash gifts or an unsought for recommendation, they get discomfited and confused about how to react. Therefore, they keep themselves in positions where people don't even know they require help. They may even cover up their lack with an apparent projection of having in excess. Even from the same partner they are codependent upon, they find it hard to take anything apart from appreciation and more requests for help.

See themselves from the eyes of other people

Codependents are some of the most self-critical individuals on earth. Their lack of self-esteem means they are forever insecure and wary of other people's opinions and perception of them. As such, they

may out up a fake lifestyle to impress people while remaining essentially hollow inwards. They do not react to negative criticism well and may either respond aggressively or go out of their way to avoid criticism entirely. Most importantly to them though, they are obsessed with how their partner views them. Does he see them as totally indispensable? Are they the only port of call when he runs into trouble again? These are the most important questions that run through the minds of codependents.

Conveniently ignore red flags

Especially in their relationships, codependent individuals always seem not to see the obvious signs. Largely inspired by their dependence on their partners and a reluctance to rock the boat or avoid conflict, they avoid fixing problems within their relationships until it is too late. They keep glossing over warning signs and refuse to heed warnings and obvious hints.

Rationalize the mistakes of others

This is the crux of codependency after all. They are always there with a readymade excuse as to why their partner isn't up to social standards. Alcoholism? Well, he had a troubled childhood. Gambling addiction? He doesn't really gamble that much. Besides, he is rich. Their library of excuses never gets exhausted. Even when the partner obviously recognizes that he has a problem that needs to be solved, they would rather remind him they are there rather than join hands to find a lasting solution.

Give more than they receive in relationships

It is constant in codependent relationships that one party gives out more care, attention and affection than the other. Individuals suffering from codependency constantly subdue the voice of their own needs, do not demand for much if anything at all and are too afraid to speak out their minds. Therefore, it is not surprising to see them constantly giving out more than they receive. Anyways, most of the time, their partners may have "bigger problems" that cries out for their attention than taking stock of the attention they receive.

Have loosely defined boundaries

Boundaries are important in every relationship. They are necessary to ensure that you don't get trampled upon. There has to be limits beyond which you won't go or tolerate. Your friends, family members and partners have to pay you some respect and not overstep their bounds. A boundary helps you mark a fine line to divide your finances, feelings, emotions and needs from that of your partner. Unfortunately, codependent relationships have undefined, poorly defined or blurred boundaries. Partners see themselves as an extension of the other half. There are no limits and invariably, emotions and desires get trampled upon. Codependents do not set boundaries because they want to remain open and be the first port of call for as many people as people when crises arise.

Say yes, all the time

A codependent does not know or use the word "NO" to any request. He never opts out of giving a service if he can, no matter the lengths he has to go to provide it. This doesn't mean that he is totally comfortable with all tasks though. He has just been configured to make himself inconvenient before he thinks of disappointing any other person. Against the backdrop of a childhood most likely spent seeking the good graces and approval of difficult parents and probably unyielding siblings, it is easy to understand why the thoughts of turning down a request might be so foreign to a codependent individual.

Feelings of guilt or responsibility for the suffering of others

The initial phase of codependency stems from a heightened sense of responsibility and duty to help other people overcome their sufferings. Especially for people who became codependent as a result of having to cater to the needs of an ill friend or relation, they become filled with the idea that they are the only ones in a unique

position to help every other person around them. Therefore, they feel heavy guilt when they are unable to stem the tide of suffering that an associate is experiencing. They see it as a failure when they are not considered to help alleviate suffering or when their ministrations fail to yield positive results. They therefore relax their boundaries and limits lower to further cater for others. Their show of care is the only thing that gives them joy and satisfaction and when people suffer, it raises a sense of guilt in them.

Reluctance to share true thoughts or feelings for fear of displeasing others

Children who grow up to be codependent are taught not to show emotions or admit weaknesses. They grow into adults incapable of intimacy. Intimacy in this instance does not refer to sexual activity although it has also been found to be affected. Intimacy in this context refers to the ability to share their feelings, emotions and desires with their partners and be capable of demanding for their rights as equal partners. Scared of displeasing people or thinking they may offend people by asking for help, they keep their true feelings within them and play to the gallery.

Chapter 9. Recovery and Healing Codependency

While codependency is a very challenging behavioral pathology, the good news is that it is definitely something that one can heal and transcend. To do this requires a strong commitment to change one's patterns of thinking and action, as well as hard work and a dependable support system. In order to make lasting changes, you must realize that the process of healing is ongoing – you will likely never reach a place where you are perfect and have no more need for improvement. However, with a sincere commitment and consistent efforts you will soon see drastic improvements that will immediately lead to a healthier and happier life.

While the road to recovery is in no way easy, it offers profound rewards and has the power to free you from much unnecessary suffering, fear, and unhappiness that you had taken to be an ordinary part of life. The truth is that codependent ways of living are not necessary and not inevitable. As you change your innermost patterns and false beliefs you may find a new life opening up for you and your close relationships.

The path to recovery from codependency we will follow in this book consists of four major steps. They are:

attaining self-awareness

healing your relationship with yourself

healing your relationship with others

opening to relationships with the world

Attaining Self-Awareness

The First Step: Acknowledgement Instead of Denial

Before one can heal themselves of a problem they must first acknowledge that there is in fact something wrong. Often this is the hardest step, and is common in virtually all cases of addiction and codependency. Denial is simply when you are unable to acknowledge or accept a truth. While you are in denial your illness will continue and you will have no hope of healing so that you can move on with living the life you desire to live.

Denial is not just a problem of the person suffering from an illness or addiction, it is also very commonly the state of one who is close to them. They deny that the other person has an illness and that this illness is negatively affecting themselves. This is a classic symptom of codependency – that you attempt to ignore the addiction or dysfunction of your partner because you are dependent on your relationship with them. As denial continues one's thoughts and behavior becomes increasingly irrational and insane, making it more and more difficult to see the reality of the situation.

One can be in denial of the continuing influence of trauma or family dysfunction because it happened in the past. They may feel that they have grown up and moved beyond it without being aware of the immense negative influence those experiences are still having on their daily life as an adult. Just because they have left the home where the issues occurred or because the addicted parent recovered does not mean that everything is healed.

Why Do We Live in Denial?

If denial served no purpose, no-one would fall under its spell. The reason why so many people live in denial is because it is a defense mechanism to protect ourselves. From our evolutionary past, our mind has learned to ignore and shut-out painful and harmful things which would prevent us from surviving; however, it becomes pathological when we ignore and prevent ourselves from seeing those things which cause us so much unnecessary suffering.

The difficulty with denial is that we don't know what we don't know. When something is unconscious we have blinded ourselves from seeing it. We can categorize the ways in which we deny reality into four categories.

The four types of denial:

Denying someone else's behavior

Denying your own codependence

Denying your own feelings

Denying your own needs

Denying someone else's behavior

This first type of denial is directed outward to someone you are in relationship with and is very common with people who struggle with codependence. You deny that they have a dysfunction and that this illness is negatively affecting you.

There are many reasons why someone may deny the behavior of another. For some they have grown up with this sort of dysfunction and so it only feels natural and they don't recognize that it is not normal. Additionally, one who has experienced this behavior their whole lives does not have an ability to trust themselves and their own perceptions and has a low self-esteem that may believe they deserve this sort of treatment. Abusers and addicts also rarely take ownership of their illness and therefore will project the blame outwards to such an extent that the person truly believes that they are at fault for the addiction of their partner.

Often times one will deny the behavior of another because they do not feel capable of facing the truth and would rather believe that it is not so bad, or that if they just pretend everything is fine the problem will resolve itself. Unfortunately, things usually just get progressively worse, and what starts out as the excusing of small issues can quickly turn into very serious behavioral problems.

It is important that you take a step back and attempt to soberly recognize if you are denying the seriousness of another's behavior. If you find yourself constantly making excuses for the behavior of others or lie and cover up things that someone you are in relationship with then you may be denying their behavior to an unhealthy extent. Additionally, if you keep changing your own needs and making concessions for the other person or keep experiencing that they are breaking promises and commitments to you than denial is likely present. Finally, if you find yourself wishing constantly that your partner, relative, or friend would change – this is a red flag that you may be living in denial rather than facing the issues in your relationship.

Denying your own codependence

The opposite of denying the problems of others is denying them in yourself. People who deny their own codependence will often blame others as an attempt to shift the responsibility away from themselves. Simply put – it is the nature of a codependent to deny their own codependence.

It can also be doubly difficult for a codependent to recognize their own dysfunction because it is the nature of codependence to focus on others at the expense of oneself. Many are simply not able to look at themselves in isolation from others but rather falsely attempt to change others in order to make themselves happy. This blaming and putting the attention upon others is done to protect you from experiencing your own pain, yet it also prevents you from taking responsibility for your life and therefore taking action to change it.

Denying your own feelings

It is an interesting irony that one who suffers from codependence is very skilled at noticing others feelings, but they know so little about their own. Someone who struggles from this form of denial finds it very difficult to feel their own feelings and understand the messages they are telling them. They will usually tell themselves and others that they are fine and nothing is bothering them.

Often this is caused from early childhood experiences which caused them to repress and suppress their feelings and pretend that everything is OK. They learn to bury their feelings because they never felt safe expressing them and this was the only way they could keep living their life without being overwhelmed by negative emotions.

The importance of allowing yourself to feel your feelings

Our feelings serve a very important purpose in that they act as our emotional compass. The way something feels to us is a very good indicator of whether it will make us happy or causes suffering. We must learn that all feeling serve a valuable purpose, even painful ones. Codependent individuals have learned to suppress their own feelings and therefore have lost this valuable emotional compass.

The following is a list of emotions and the message they have to teach us:

Sadness can teach us the preciousness of life and the importance of compassion and empathy. A life without sadness would also be unable to experience joy.

Fear warns us of danger and of things that may harm us. It also serves to show us what part of ourselves and our life we are unwilling to experience.

Anger is a message that something you are experiencing is unjustified and in pills us to make a change or correct an injustice. It is also one possible expression of fear.

Guilt is a signal that we have done something that goes against our values and our inner integrity.

Loneliness is a message to connect with others and change how you view your relationship to life.

Shame is similar to guilt in that it tells us that we have done something we should not have done.

The problem with suppressing and hiding one's feelings is that that energy cannot be hidden and gotten rid of, it must be expressed in some manner. Different people will have different ways of letting loose this tension and trapped energy. Some will hold it in for a while and then explode when the pressure becomes too much. Others will attempt to eat their emotions with food or substitute them with drunks. Others will internalize this negative energy and manifest illnesses and physical pains. One way or another your emotions and feelings must be honored, acknowledged, and felt or they were only rear their head at a later time and cause more suffering.

Denying your own needs

Just as codependents are good at feeling others emotions but not their own, they are also in the same way skilled at acknowledging others needs at the expense of their own. Once again due to early childhood experiences some people never learn that they are entitled to certain basic needs for their safety and well-being. Also, someone may have had all of their material needs met but none of their emotional or spiritual needs satisfied. This person may believe that all their needs are met, but this is only because they do not know what they are missing because they have never experienced it.

At the other end of the spectrum, a codependent may become a tyrant to expects everyone to for fill their needs. Rather than denying their own needs, they over-exaggerate them and create needs that are not truly needs but more closely wants and greedy desires.

When parents create a safe space for their children to convey their needs and desires they grow into adults who are likewise comfortable asking for what they need. However, when adults ridicule children who ask for things they need the child learns that it is better to just be quiet and deny their need. The person who recognizes their codependent tendencies must learn that it is perfectly normal to be vulnerable and express your needs in your relationships.

How to overcome denial

While denial can be very difficult to recognize, the key is to understand that by seeing the truth of what is going on without sweeping it under the rug will not cause you more pain. You must change your perception to the understanding that it is only your belief that makes something appear to be fearful and painful. The truth is that when you recognize the true reality and take actions to alter your behavior you will only feel better. In understanding that the recognition of your sickness will allow you to heal it and won't cause more pain, then you will be free to acknowledge the full reality of your situation. Once you have done this you are empowered to make changes.

The Willingness to Change

The very fact that you are reading this book is a very good sign because it means that you deeply care about changing yourself or helping someone you loved change. Therefore, this all-important willingness to change is already in-progress.

It is important for us to acknowledge that while we may wish to change, often change can be very challenging because we have grown so comfortable in our patterns - even if they are dysfunctional and keeping us from happiness. The willingness to change includes the understanding that we will become a new person through this transformation from codependence to individual sovereignty. We won't however become someone we dislike; we will become more of our true, natural self who we always have longed to be.

The willingness to change comes easy when we clearly recognize how our codependent patterns and habits are causing us to suffer. And as we have already discussed, once we move past denial and false beliefs that it will be difficult and painful to change - then we can experience the fun and feeling of accomplishment that comes from improving ourselves.

Most important of all is truly believing that you can change. This is really the first and last step. Those who do not change either do not want to change; or if they do, they don't actually believe that it is possible.

Commitment

Along with having the willingness to make deep, radical, and lasting changes in your life is the importance of commitment. Ending and transforming patter1 as you are seeing things about yourself that you do not like and experiencing emotions that you have spent your whole life avoiding.

Also, in order for the commitment to be strong enough to last you must make this commitment with yourself. You may be seeking help at the request of someone else or in order to repair a relationship, but you must realize that this is a self-commitment and you are doing this first and foremost for yourself. For it is only when you are healthy that you can truly help others and participate in balanced relationships. Those who seek healing only to appease another are still caught within the codependent mindset of putting others needs before your own. In order for the change to last the commitment must come from within.

Finding Help

Now that you have a strong desire to change and are fully committed, the next step is to find sources of support and methods to aid you in your recovery. It is recommended that you seek aid outside of your family and friendships, this is because it is often these very relationships and family setting that is supporting your codependent tendencies. However, if you have friends that you trust and can be sure that your relationship with them is healthy and balanced, then these people can be valuable supporters in your journey.

Support

It is highly recommended that you find external sources of support. All too often individuals try to 'go it alone' and as a result have no- one to confide in, to encourage them, and to help them stay focused on their goals. Not to mention the fact that this way of operating falls right into the comfort zone of those with the codependent patterns of trying to do everything alone and be self-sufficient.

If possible, it is recommended that you obtain the support of those who have experience with codependency. Perhaps they are an experienced therapist, a trained counselor, or a Twelve Step group. With the proliferation of the internet there are many online support groups; just keep in mind that while you may receive great comfort from having a community who understands what you are going through, some of the advice you receive may not be accurate for your situation.

Two of the most effective methods of support are to be found in therapy sessions and in group meetings. We recommend partaking in both of these practices simultaneously for a good mix of techniques and help in your recovery. For instance, you can participate in a Twelve Step group while taking psychotherapy sessions with a professional therapist. Each of these alone can be very effective, and when combined they provide two very different approaches to healing.

The Twelve Step Model

The Twelve Step model has become a very powerful method for people of all types of addictions to find a path to recovery. Originally started for alcoholics, the process is a universal one for all types of addictions and compulsive behavior. As already discussed, codependency is a type of addiction and the Twelve Steps is a powerful process that if followed leads one from being a victim to their compulsions and unconscious behavior to being a free and autonomous individual.

Co-dependents Anonymous is the Twelve Step program specifically for codependent individuals. At these meetings you will be able to listen to speakers, discuss different literature on codependence, and share your experiences. The encouragement you will find at one of these meetings is one of the most beneficial aspects. Many recovering codependents feel isolated and the camaraderie and friendship you can find with others who are struggling with the same issues is critically important. The shared experiences you are exposed to at these meetings can inspire you because you have seen others find healing from the same struggles. As a part of this program you will receive a sponsor, who is someone you can go to for guidance and support throughout your journey. Additionally, the meetings are completely free and totally anonymous. You do not need to worry about being able to afford them or the people in your life finding out that you are attending them if you do not wish them too.

Central to the Twelve Step philosophy is a belief in surrender to a higher power. This does not necessarily mean that you need to be religious to participate. Your conception of this higher power could be aligned with a major religion or with a general spiritual outlook, or even atheist as long as you are willing to acknowledge that there is a greater power than your ego in the universe.

Co-Dependents Anonymous

The only requirement for membership in Co-dependents Anonymous or CoDA is a desire to have loving relationships and move beyond personal histories and codependent behaviors. The Twelve Steps are a proven process that aid you in living from your true, natural Self, instead of from your ego that is controlled by fear and desire.

Psychotherapy

A source of help that many find very useful on their journey of recovery is to have sessions with a psychotherapist. There are many licensed mental health professionals who specialize on treating codependency and addiction. It is recommended that you check any possible therapists to make sure that they have a degree and credentials as well as that they are experienced working with codependent individuals.

Meeting with a therapist can be helpful in many ways. While Twelve Steps groups can be very good for someone seeking to heal codependency, they do not offer individual attention that is vital to be able to go deeply into your beliefs, experiences, feelings, and particular situation. Your therapist should be an expert and experienced mentor who can also act as an objective guide to you in the very challenging process of change. Also, therapy sessions are intimate and private – allowing you to remove your masks and protections and open up in a one-on-one setting with someone who is not a friend or family member. This often allows people to be more open and honest. With a skilled psychotherapist it is possible to go deeper into the root issues that have been bothering you your whole life. Additionally, some people find the inherently spiritual tone of the Twelve Step program to be not to their liking, psychotherapy is more scientific and need not include any spirituality.

Chapter 10. Establishing Independence

A person may choose to end a life of codependency for any number of reasons. However, even though these reasons may differ in appearance they usually boil down to two main goals. The first goal is to escape the abuse that comes from a codependent relationship. As already discussed, such abuse can take on several forms, including physical, emotional and psychological. The need to be free from abuse of any kind is often enough to motivate a person to free themselves from any codependent relationships they find themselves in. The second goal that inspires a person to escape codependency is to establish independence. When a person is trapped in a codependent relationship they spend their life serving the needs and desires of others. Once that person decides they want to spend their life in pursuit of their personal goals and ambitions it becomes necessary to escape any and all codependent relationships. Only then can the individual be free from the burden of serving others and begin to live a life for themselves, one that enables them to pursue their dreams and find the happiness they deserve. This chapter will discuss several methods for establishing the independence needed to live the free and fulfilling life that awaits the person who escapes the bonds of codependency.

Define yourself as an individual

The first step toward establishing independence is to begin defining yourself as an individual. Anyone who lives their life in codependence will acquire a self-image that is akin to a hive mentality. Rather than being a single person with personal feelings, thoughts, dreams and goals they see themselves as part of a collective. Even if that collective is comprised of only two people it is still enough to see the individual lose all sense of individuality. Instead, they take on the needs and desires of the taker, who dominates the relationship, thereby defining the nature of all involved. This hive-like mindset can be very difficult to break, especially for someone who has spent years in a codependent environment. However, it is absolutely vital that it not only be broken, but that it is replaced with an independent mindset, one that is healthy and strong and enables the individual to retake control of their life.

One of the first things you need to do when shifting from a shared mindset to an individual mindset is to list all of your current thoughts, feelings, dreams and goals on a piece of paper. Needless to say, most of these thoughts, feelings, dreams and goals will not necessarily be yours at this point. Rather, they are probably the contents left over from any codependent relationships you recently liberated yourself from. This is why it is important to list them on a piece of paper. Once you have created your list the next step is to identify each individual entry as something that belongs to you or something that comes from the heart and mind of someone else. How you mark the items on your list is up to you, the important thing is that you clearly differentiate those things that are yours from those things that aren't. You can put an "x" next to the items that don't come from your heart and mind, and a check mark next to those things that do. Alternatively, you can cross off the items that are alien, leaving your thoughts, hopes and dreams unmarked. In the end, all that matters is that you do what feels best to you.

The next step is to take the items that made the cut, namely those items that belong to you, and create a new list. This new list will be the start of your new life, one that is focused on chasing those dreams that come from your heart and mind, not the heart and mind of another person. You may find a very small number of items on this list, and that shouldn't concern you. The real aim of this exercise isn't to discover your dreams, rather it is to differentiate them from those dreams that don't belong to you. Once you make this distinction you can clear your heart and mind of the ambitions that came from others, thereby making room for those hopes and desires that are yours and yours alone. This will enable you to focus your energies on those things that will bring happiness and meaning into your life, thus creating the life you deserve.

Discover your personal hopes and dreams

After you have cleared your mind of the thoughts, hopes, desires and dreams that weren't yours you can begin to fill it with those that truly do belong to you. However, most people at this stage struggle to come up with a list of any significance, both in terms of length as well as in terms of substance. The few items they can list out usually seem fairly trivial, especially compared to the grandiose schemes that they had been expected to fulfill on behalf of the taker in their codependent relationships. This is perfectly normal, as anyone who has been in a codependent relationship will have turned their mind off to anything that was self-serving and focused their attention and efforts instead on things that served the taker in the relationship. More often than not the average giver doesn't have the time or the motivation to contemplate personal goals, therefore they find that their mind is blank when they go to write out any personal goals or dreams once they achieve their freedom from codependency. Therefore, at this point you need to take the time to actually discover those things that you want to do now that your life is yours once again.

The first step to discovering your hopes and dreams is to sit down and ask yourself one simple question, "If I could do anything with my life, what would I do?" Some people struggle to find any answers at all to this question at first. Again, this is particularly true for anyone who has spent a great deal of time as a giver in a codependent relationship. In this case the trick is to give yourself the time you need to find the answers. It may come down to spending time in the outside world in order to find inspiration and ideas. After all, most victims of codependent relationships live very sheltered and controlled lives. Therefore, they don't always know the options that are available to them when it comes to creating an independent life. The important thing is to take all the time you need to find what inspires you. Once you find inspiration, be sure to write it down so that you can start pursuing that goal and finding the happiness that you deserve.

Alternatively, some people find that they have many ideas and dreams to put down in their list. The problem most of these people face is that many of those ideas and dreams seem totally unrealistic, as though they are the product of an overly active imagination. This may in fact be true to a large degree, since many victims of codependent relationships create a vivid fantasy world in which they can escape the pain and suffering they experience in their real life. It can be all too tempting to not write down such dreams and ideas, dismissing them as too unrealistic or ridiculous to admit, let alone consider pursuing. However, it is vital that you write down every idea and dream that you have, no matter how fantastic or unrealistic it may be. The objective here isn't to create your life plan, instead it is simply to discover your innermost hopes and desires. Therefore, write down any and every dream you have, even if it is to become king or queen of the world!

Once you have written this list it is important to go over it and make sure that all of your entries pass the requirement of belonging to you and not to someone else. There is always the chance that some of the old thoughts and dreams from codependent relationships are still floating around in your mind, pretending to belong to you when in fact they don't. Therefore, go over your list item by item, making sure that everything you have written down reflects who you are as an independent person and not the subservient person you once were. If you find any items that don't belong cross them out completely, both from the list and from your mind. Tell yourself that those things aren't a part of your life anymore, and that they have no place in your thoughts. Breaking free from the influences of codependency can take a lot more time and effort than most people realize. Therefore, always be sure to take all the time and effort you need to achieve true and lasting freedom. Only then can you live a life that brings you true joy and meaning.

Determine your direction

Now that you have compiled a list of your own personal hopes and dreams you can begin to take the next step, that of determining your direction. Depending on what your dreams and goals are you might only need to consider getting a better job or a better place to live. These things won't necessarily be overly complicated, and the direction you need to establish in order to achieve them will be fairly straight forward. However, in the event that you want to change your life in more profound ways, such as leaving the town or city in which you live, getting a better education, training for a new career, or even something more profound such as entering politics, you will need to steer your life in a precise direction, one that leads you away from your codependent past and toward your newfound life-goal.

The important thing here isn't to create a goal simply for the sake of creating a goal. Instead, it is to create a goal that will bring the most happiness and meaning into your life. This is why it is important to create a clear list of all of your hopes and dreams. This list will present certain patterns, and it is those patterns that will determine the direction you need to take in order to achieve the life of your dreams. For some people the list will consist largely of things oriented around a job or career. Whether it's about making more money, finding a job that is more challenging, or pursuing the career of your dreams, in this case your direction will be job-oriented. This means that you need to spend your time and efforts pursuing everything you need in order to get that dream job, including training, education, and even contacts who might help you to get your foot in the proverbial door.

Alternatively, your list might consist of items of a different nature, such as making friends, finding a person to share your life with, or even starting a family. If the pattern of your list is more about love and friendship than of money and a career then you need to steer your life in the appropriate direction. Rather than spending all of your time fixated on your job or your finances you need to spend your time and efforts socializing. Start spending time with any friends you currently have, especially in such settings as parties or social gatherings where you can meet new people. By exposing yourself to more people you can start to make new friends, or even start looking to engage in relationships of a more intimate nature. The key is to break out of the bubble you lived in as a victim of codependency and begin to expand your social and romantic horizons. If love and friendship is where you will find happiness then you need to make those your new priorities in life.

While getting a better job and making more friends is all that it takes to bring meaning and happiness to most people, you might find that you need something else in order to erase the memories and influences of your codependent past. Perhaps you dreamed of being something extraordinary, such as a scientist, an author, or a world famous chef. In all likelihood you gave up getting the education you would need to achieve such goals in order to be in the relationship that turned out to be codependent in the end. Now that you are free from any and all codependent relationships you can start chasing those dreams that you sacrificed in the past. In this case you will want to spend your time and effort discovering what it will take to turn those dreams into reality. Whether it's as simple as an online course, or maybe something more complicated, such as getting a graduate degree, the important thing is to determine the direction you need to go in order to move closer to achieving your life's ambitions.

Create a plan

Once you have determined the direction your life needs to take in order to become the happy and fulfilling life you both desire and deserve, the next and final step to achieving independence is to create a plan. While determining a direction and creating a plan may seem to be one and the same at first they are actually two distinctly different processes. The process of determining direction allows you to come up with the overall goal that will bring happiness into your life. This is the general idea as it were. In contrast, creating a plan is the process of laying out a step-by-step approach that will enable you to achieve your goal.

A good analogy of this is the planning of a vacation. When you plan a vacation the first thing you do is decide the type of vacation you want. You might want to spend a week hiking in the woods, skiing in the mountains, or just lounging around on a beach. Deciding the type of vacation you want is the same thing as determining the direction in your life. The next step is to choose a specific destination, and thus plan on how you will get there. You might need to book a flight if your destination is a long way off. If your destination is closer to home you might only need to choose the route you will drive in order to get to where you want to be. This is the process of creating a plan.

If getting a better job is all that it will take to make your life a happy and content one then the plan would be to look around at all of the jobs that are available. If any of them jump out at you then you move to the next phase, namely filling out any necessary applications or other paperwork and pursuing an interview. The important thing is to focus all of your time and energy on achieving your goal, being sure to take each of the necessary steps carefully and thoughtfully, thereby giving yourself the best chance of success. Researching the best methods for creating resumes or taking interviews, for example, might be another step you take in order to increase your chances of success.

In the event that you don't find any of the available jobs appealing you will want to figure out what job you are looking for. Next, decide what companies or locations would offer that type of job and begin to visit those places. Try to get an appointment with someone in charge of hiring who can advise you on when jobs might become available and on the things you will need when applying for those jobs. This will give you a head start, one that might make the difference when it comes to landing the job of your dreams. Again, the important thing is to create a plan that will take you toward your goal.

Finally, if you are the type of person who requires something greater than a regular job or the happiness that friends or a family can provide, then you will need to create a more intricate and lengthy plan, one that will launch you from the shallows of your codependent past into the stratosphere of your ultimate dreams.

Such a plan will doubtlessly involve the pursuit of higher education. Even before you start applying to colleges and universities the first thing you will probably need to do is determine the finances you need for such an education. The next step will be to look for scholarships, grants and loans that will provide the funds you need to for your higher education. After all, there is no point in applying to a college if you can't actually afford to go.

All of these intricate details are the nuts and bolts that go into creating a plan. Sometimes, when you get into the planning phase the details can seem too complicated, pushing your dream out of reach. Fortunately, there are usually websites or people who can coach you on how to effectively create your plan, especially one of a more complex nature. This goes back to the concept of knowing when to ask for help. If you feel overwhelmed when trying to create the plan that will take you to the life of your dreams, rather than simply giving up or putting forth a half-hearted attempt find someone who can help you to create the plan that will enable you to achieve your goal. Always remember that you deserve the life of your dreams, therefore you are worth every effort that is required for turning those dreams into reality.

Chapter 11. Cultivating Self-love

One of the most powerful things you can do for yourself when finding yourself in a toxic or codependent relationship is to practice self-love. Self-love can be achieved and attained in many ways and some have already been explored throughout these chapters. Let's look at the many ways to cultivate self-love. You can use this as a guide and find a creative way to make sure you include some on a daily basis (tarot-style cards, a self-love journal...).

Take time for yourself. Do what you love doing!

Follow your passions. Stay committed to your goals, dreams and aspirations.

Lose the need to please and appease. Recondition your mind.

Meditate on self-love and incorporate daily mantras into your life.

Look after your physical health. Vitality and love for your physical body can help keep you strong and -ed within.

Look after your emotional health. Put up healthy boundaries on your emotions and do not allow harm into your energy field.

Look after your mental health. Keep your mind focused and aligned to your truth, your inner knowing and your own peace of mind.

Look after your spiritual health. Remind yourself daily how wise, loving, empathic and connected you are; and that you are a beautiful, soulful being.

Spend time in nature. Connect to nature to help cultivate self-love and remind yourself of your personal power, beauty and greatness.

Strengthen your boundaries.

Be kinder to yourself. Treat yourself with loving kindness.

Remind yourself of your independence.

Develop your intuition.

Practice forgiveness.

Take time for self-reflection, journaling and explorations of your self and psyche.

Balance your masculine and feminine energy.

Meditate on the moon. The moon relates to your emotions and divine feminine wisdom. Connect to her.

Let go of the need to compare yourself to others.

Self-care. Incorporate healing massage, self-pampering and other self-loving rituals into daily life.

Create a sacred space. Create a shrine, altar or sacred space with items that can help you connect to your inner nature and develop self-love.

Live intentionally. Apply meaning to daily life.

Cultivating Self-Compassion

Just like self-love, having compassion for self is essential when dealing with manipulative narcissists or any other toxic personalities. It is also extremely important if you yourself are suffering from any codependent tendencies and destructive cycles of behavior. Without self-compassion, we would not be able to experience compassion for others. Compassion literally translates as 'the concern for the suffering of others' therefore being compassionate, for self and others, can have some profound effects.

Here are 7 things you should do to help bring greater compassion into your life.

Charity or animal welfare - One of the most powerful ways to increase our self-confidence and remind ourselves of our true intentions and compass is to help others. When we engage in an activity that enhances another's life, our hearts begin to glow and our inner confidence rockets. For those of you suffering from issues such as self-esteem or any feelings of inadequacy, helping others takes the focus away from you and your perceived follies and shifts your awareness onto others.

Create a vision or manifestation board - Linking with number 1 is our sense of personal goals, dreams and aspirations. A lack of compassion for ourselves primarily stems from an inability to put ourselves first, have self-love and follow our own inner desires. Creating and making steps to align to a vision or manifestation board can really help increase your confidence and sense of self. Related strongly with this is step 3.

Develop healthy boundaries - This is essential and I cannot stress this enough. Having healthy boundaries is one of the most significant things you can do to help alleviate the strains of codependency. When we have no boundaries, we literally lose our sense of self. When dealing with narcissists, abusers, control freaks, energy vampires, cynics, any toxic person or any of the harmful forms of communication, boundaries can arguably be seen as fundamental to the health and sanity of the partner in a codependent relationship. In the last section of this chapter is a step by step guide of how to develop your own boundaries within.

Cultivate compassion - Cultivating compassion through meditation, mindfulness or mantras is a highly effective practice to help break the cycle or chains of codependency. These activities can all be used to reshape and restructure your inner workings, detrimental emotional patterns and deeply ingrained beliefs which may be preventing compassion for self or others to shine through. Make a daily habit of consciously taking the effort to cultivate compassion and you will witness just how much better you feel and how much more able you are to respond to situations with compassion, ease and grace.

Connect to universal symbolism.- Connecting to universal symbolism can be very useful in reshaping and activating certain neurological activity and codons in the brain. As our brains are just transmitters and receivers of consciousness -they don't create consciousness itself -there are many universal symbols and archetypes that can be tuned in to for a healing effect. The Buddha for example represents the embodiment of universal love and compassion. There are many people who recognize the energy of the Buddha without actually being religious or Buddhist themselves. Connecting to symbols which represent compassion therefore can really aid in your journey to recovery and inner peace.

Learn to laugh.- Learning to laugh can be a very profound self-help when trying to overcome codependency and welcome more compassion into your life. This is because laughter literally releases emotions and blocked energy. Any repressed feelings, thoughts, stories, scenarios or memories which have been pushed down and are literally holding you down can come up through laughter. Being compassionate with yourself is essentially being kind to yourself and recognizing that you deserve to be free from pain and suffering. Laughter is a very powerful way to do this! Make a conscious effort to laugh more or incorporate conscious laughter exercises into daily life such as laughter yoga.

Recognize that everyone is a reflection.- We are all mirrors of one another and your partner is you in essence. When you recognize that we all wish to be happy, healthy and free from suffering, you will begin to treat yourself the loving kindness that you deserve. Whether your intentions are for you or for another, recognizing the inner connection and shared humanity will help you profoundly on your journey to wholeness. Take time to reflect, journal and meditate on the interconnected nature of life and be conscious of the thoughts and beliefs you project both internally and externally.

Cultivating compassion through any of these ways will allow you to have the self- love and respect necessary to move on from your codependent relationship, break the cycle and, when you are ready, find new love. Compassion can also help you recognize the importance of your own health, on all levels. Your mental, emotional, physical and spiritual health are all equally important and some things may not be that obvious or known until you truly begin to develop the self- compassion necessary.

Linking in to habitual and compulsive thinking is the importance of habit or routine. Here is an example compassion routine you can include into your day. Each only takes a few minutes, but the effects are extremely powerful and can vastly expand your self- awareness and ability to attract only loving, supportive and harmonious relationships and interactions into your life.

Morning Self- Compassion Routine

Upon waking, speak some mantras or positive affirmations to yourself. When you first wake up you are essentially a blank canvas, despite whatever personal stories and realities you have going on. Self- affirmations can fill you up with positive stories and rewire your mind for a loving and supportive day. These affirmations may include: "Today is a new day. I am loved, loveable and capable of giving love." "My mind is beautiful. I have a happy heart and positive outlook."

Engage in some mirror work - Mirror work is also known as eye gazing and can really help cultivate positive, loving and self- compassionate feelings towards yourself. Look at your own reflection and see the beauty of your soul or psyche. Speak supporting and positive words to yourself, and know within that you are worthy of the best love and life. Take no shame in this- embrace the confidence and self- esteem you find yourself exhibiting. Mirror work is powerful.

Do something self- caring - Self- care is very helpful for cultivating compassion and can involve pampering, massage or any joyous activity or hobby. You may have a love of yoga or dancing or you may enjoy gardening or working in some way with essential oils or flower essences. Do something for you, and don't feel guilty in the process.

Eat healthily - Incorporating superfood smoothies into your day can really help enhance your mood, self- esteem and love for yourself. Your body, mind and emotions are said to work in synergy, therefore loving your body can only have a positive effect on your mind and emotional wellbeing. Cacao is a really powerful superfood to include as it is high in antioxidants and can improve heart and brain health. It is essentially raw chocolate and has the feel good factors of normal chocolate, amplified!

Care for a plant - Introducing plants to your home can bring greater feelings of love and connection, and also provide the sense of caring for another. Purchase plants that can be seen as a reflection of you in some way such as a Japanese peace lily, aloe vera or money plant. The first brings deep feelings of peace and acceptance, the second is known as the healing plant and the latter is known to bring luck and abundance.

Journal - Expressing yourself each morning such as by writing down your dreams, writing in your journal or creating a list of goals and intentions can really help steer you in the right direction for your day ahead. These activities allow for honesty and authentic expression of your feelings, emotions and thoughts and simultaneously increase positive feelings through the acceptance and release writing brings. They can also help you see yourself clearly and in a non- judgemental and compassionate way.

Developing Awareness

Developing awareness is important in the journey to recovery from a toxic or unhealthy codependent relationship (or if you are recovering from codependent tendencies yourself). Without awareness, we would not be able to feel, experience, see, observe, sense or understand life and all its many elements. If our judgment is clouded, our overall vision for life is blurred. This results in us attracting characters and situations that aren't particularly good for our health.

Let's look at the ways in which we can develop awareness and break the cycle of codependency for good.

Binaural beats

Because binaural beats are very influential and can have some real profound effects of developing awareness, increasing confidence and improving aspects of life in so many ways, we will explore all the various binaural beats in depth.

Binaural beats are frequencies of sound which -when heard - have a specific effect on the listener's consciousness. This means that the sound waves played actively alter neurological activity and structures in the brain. Neurons of course have a direct effect on our emotions, daily thoughts, ingrained beliefs, wellbeing and passion and love for life. Incorporating binaural beats into everyday reality therefore will not only expand your awareness but can also provide you direct insight and wisdom into how to deal with toxic or harmful energy, making life so much easier and full of bliss.

Let's explore these in detail.

0.1-4 Hz. This frequency is also known as Delta. It is responsible for deep sleep, pain relief, reduction of cortisol (anti-aging) and accessing the unconscious mind. Delta waves can be played to increase healing, access the unconscious mind and exploring wounds and traumas leading to insight.

4-8 Hz, the Theta frequency. This is where REM sleep occurs and deep states of inner peace and calmness are induced. Theta frequencies can therefore be listened to enhance states of deep inner peace and relaxation, enhance meditation, increase creativity and develop hypersensitive states.

8-14 Hz. This frequency is Alpha and corresponds with stress reduction, relaxation and relaxed focus, positive thinking, advanced and accelerated learning, and states of natural flow. Connecting to alpha therefore can help with all of the things mentioned in addition

to allowing you to effortlessly engage with your environment through the increased mental states.

14-30 Hz, Beta frequency. Beta is your sense of focused intention. It relates to high level cognitive functioning, analytical thinking, problem solving and it stimulates energy, vitality, mental awareness and action. Listening to these frequencies can be used to enhance and connect to all of these qualities.

30-100 Hz. This is the Gamma frequency range. Tuning into gamma will aid in high levels of information processing, help attune your mind to receive wisdom and insights from an external or higher source, enhance cognitive abilities, aid in memory recall and help you reach heightened states of awareness. Gamma also relates to transcendental meditation states and altered states of consciousness therefore can be listened to develop an inner bliss, calmness and contentment whilst simultaneously stimulating your mind and mental powers.

As you can see, each frequency range has a specific effect therefore using binaural beats to aid in your journey to recovery can act as a daily meditation and stimulation into action.

Journal

As listed in 'Cultivating Self-love' journaling and self-reflective measures are an effective way to overcome codependency and release yourself from limiting or self-sabotaging behaviors. When we write, we are free to express. When we express, we release. When we release we can finally move forward, leaving behind detrimental stories, attachments and belief systems. Journaling can also act as a form of forgiveness as you are directly taking the steps to let go, release and move on. This in itself leads to greater awareness of self, others and life experiences and situations which have shaped your own unique individual journey.

Intuitive, psychic and spiritual development

Intuitive, psychic and spiritual development is a topic that is not explored on a mass scale or taught in mainstream education however thousands if not millions are recognizing the importance of developing their own inner intuition and awakening to subtle levels of perception. Intuition is not exclusive with spirituality and psychic phenomena however they are related. When one opens to their inner knowing and attunes their mind to higher levels of awareness, cognitive functioning and perception, this naturally opens them up to a more subtle and spiritual way of perceiving.

Spirituality is simply recognizing the interconnected nature of life. We are all one and ultimately we all wish to be treated with love, kindness and respect and experience connection, intimacy, friendship and joy on a daily basis. Closing ourselves off to these beautiful and essential elements of life therefore (through allowing toxic and harmful energy to prevent these from manifesting) also closes off our intuition, our sense of inner knowing. Taking steps to develop psychic and spiritual energy or perception can aid greatly in all aspects of both life and relationships.

Let's explore some of these ways.

Learn about Astrology - Learning about the planets, stars and universe and cosmos as a whole can help you to expand your psychic and spiritual awareness. This because we are intrinsically connected to 'all that is' and life is not just limited to our one world on planet earth. Learning about and connecting to other planets, star systems and universal phenomena can help you feel more connected, safe and secure in your body and physical environments.

Practice a healing art - Learning and training in a healing art such as Reiki, energy healing or holistic massage can have a profound effect on your conscious awareness and general wellbeing. Feeling connected to others and the world around, and your own inner state of self-confidence and assuredness, is an effective way to help deal with any problems in codependent relationships. There are many healing systems and schools of thought to choose from so do some research and see what feels right for you.

Explore your subconscious - Looking to our shadow can shine some light on where we may be going wrong and why. In addition to looking towards philosophical schools of thought such as yin and yang, Taoist philosophy and collective issues regarding sexuality, explore the teachings of Carl Jung. Jung was a Swiss psychiatrist who went on to become one of the founding fathers of modern psychology. He came up with a set of universal archetypes which are inherent within every human being. These archetypes can be learned about and explored to understand the psyche and elements of our own human nature, beliefs, repression, shadow and self. Take time to reflect and do some soul searching.

Practice mindfulness - Practicing mindfulness specifically on developing qualities associated with your third eye, intuition and spiritual perception can be very beneficial. Learning how to shift your thoughts, beliefs and viewpoints to one more interconnected and 'seeing' will not only bring greater awareness but also aid in your ability to put up barriers and protect yourself. Your boundaries will become stronger, confidence will increase and very simply you will learn how to say no to the bullsh*t!

Decalcify your pineal gland - Decalcifying your pineal gland can lead greatly to the ability to see and perceive subtle energy and therefore interact with others in a way more loving and harmonious to you. The pineal gland is a real gland which also relates to psychic and spiritual phenomena. When it is clouded, we are closed off from many extrasensory aspects of life. There are more than the five physical senses and those with an active and open pineal gland are aware of this. To decalcify your' pineal, follow these steps:

1-Do a 3 day water cleanse. This will flush and cleanse your system and your pineal gland of any toxins and harmful chemicals.

2-Eat lots of greens like spinach, kale, broccoli, and other vegetables.

3-Perform aura strengthening exercises and work on your intuition. Any exercise which actively helps strengthen your pineal gland is great.

4-Cultivate self-love and compassion. As spirituality is strongly connected to the heart and a sense of universal and unconditional love, cultivating self- love and compassion will have a positive effect on your pineal gland.

5-Finally include binaural beats and sound healing exercises into your day. The range of effects are immense and will help open you up to psychic and subtler ways of perceiving, sensing and relating.

There are also many psychological approaches to developing awareness however a lot of these involve seeing qualified and experienced therapists. Hypnotherapy and past- life regression therapy are two profound avenues for the recovery of codependency, as is any form of psychotherapy or analysis.

Hypnotherapy can have a very powerful effect as hypnosis allows you to explore aspects of your unconscious mind you may not have been aware of. This in turn can 'spark' or trigger certain elements of your subconscious and bring them to light for healing and integration. You may not have previously been aware that you held a block or aversion to something and therefore discovering this would allow for the block to be released and a real shift to take place in daily life.

Past- life regression therapy is similar but it goes a step further and enables you to get to the root of hidden aspects of yourself relating to your childhood or past experiences. These memories are then connected to and brought to the surface, opening up a portal of consciousness for your relationship and personal problem areas.

Let's look at the positive benefits of these in bullet point form so you can decide for yourself whether you feel they will be helpful for you.

Hypnotherapy/ hypnosis:

It can help improve your mood, ease depression and release tension or nervous anxiety.

It induces deep feelings of relaxation and inner calm.

It can help release limiting thoughts, beliefs and behaviors.

It can allow you to explore aspects of your unconscious and subconscious mind you didn't know were available.

It can enhance creativity, passion and imagination therefore steering you onto new paths and pursuits.

It can alter the way you think and perceive based on the triggering of certain subconscious aspects.

It can generally lead to a more positive outlook on life. Past-life regression therapy:

It can help overcome fears and phobias.

It can help heal relationships and your attitude towards them.

It can help you overcome any blocks to happiness and health.

It can increase compassion and a sense of love in your life.

It can help release any karmic ties or contracts on a deeper, spiritual level.

It can help with mental and emotional problems.

It can provide clarity of thought and a deeper understanding of your life.

It can help release limiting thoughts, beliefs and behaviors.

It can create a lightness, release you from strains of the past and release fear for your future.

Changes in perspective can occur as can new wisdoms and ways of thinking.

Self- esteem, confidence and self- worth can increase.

Creating Healthy Boundaries Within

As you are aware by now, boundaries are essential when dealing with any toxic personality or attempting to overcome the destructive patterns of a codependent relationship. All of life on earth including ourselves is interconnected. We are not separate from one another.

Thoughts, feelings, emotions, beliefs, and intentions all swirl around in an energetic spiral rippling out to affect everything our intended awareness is directed at. When someone aims harm, anger, sadness, pain, suffering or any negative and harmful thought or intention towards you, you respond. We are transmitters and receivers of both consciousness and external sensory stimuli therefore when recovering from codependency, it is fundamental to take steps to protect yourself. This could possibly be the greatest lesson and most powerful thing you do for yourself on your journey to healing and wholeness.

As all life on earth is governed by unseen, energetic forces and science has shown nowadays how we ourselves have an electromagnetic energy field surrounding us responsible for our thoughts, emotions, feelings and overall state of wellbeing and energetic frequency (also known as the aura to some), the best way to develop healthy boundaries within is to practice daily exercises and techniques for strengthening your energy field and putting up a shield.

This final section will guide you through practical and highly accessible steps to do so.

Strengthen your inner chi!

Martial artists and many who practice hands on or energy healing are aware of the subtle yet powerful chi which flows through us. Chi flows through every living thing on earth -the trees, earth, plants, waters, sky, sun, sea, your hands, your feet and your entire body. It is in the crops we eat and the air we breathe. Without chi, we would not exist.

Chi is also referred to as the universal life force. It is an energetic force, similar to air and oxygen as both are breathed in simultaneously however chi also has metaphysical properties which can be tuned in to and embodied for healing.

Your chi is very much connected to your ability to fight off disease, your inner strength, health and physical vitality. It is also responsible for your emotional health, mental health and spiritual holistic wellbeing. Without chi -the life force energy -our immune systems would become weak, the mind clouded and our intuition -our inner knowing suppressed. Just like martial artists cultivate chi to do some incredible things, we too can. For the purpose of our intentions, we will be developing chi to aid in the journey to recovery and wholeness.

Chi balls are fascinating to try and also really fun. Creating chi balls has some incredible effects. A chi ball can be created to increase mental powers, increase focus, expand awareness, heal your chakras, heal emotions, energize any particular area of your body, mind or inner being, develop intuition and send loving energy to the heart. This is because when we create a chi ball, we are literally 'creating a ball of chi' which can then be sent anywhere we desire. For example, say you are suffering from always believing the lies of a compulsive liar and your intuition is beginning to come into question. You can create a (powerful) ball of chi, set your intention and send it to your brow chakra. Your brow or third eye chakra will then become energized as you have enabled a freer flow of energy to that centre and all its corresponding associations. The same can be done for any aspect of self.

When we create chi balls, this natural strengthens our aura and unseen barriers (boundaries, electromagnetic energy field) as we are filling ourselves up with more chi and strengthening many aspects of self. Due to the effect chi balls have on the mind, they also increase mental powers, calmness and clarity which can help in any situation when you need boundaries with a toxic person. It is so simple yet so effective.

Chi balls can be connected to in any time or place and can help with any situation. They are very powerful!

Diet

As your chi is your life force, changing your diet to one high in life force foods will have an incredibly profound effect on your ability to protect yourself and put up better boundaries. Fruits, nuts, seeds, whole grains, vegetables, lentils and pulses, beans, herbs, herbal teas and organic wholefoods are all foods high in life force. As all food on earth whether that be vegetables, pasta or beef receive their energy directly from the elements of nature. These foods however hold a higher vibration. This is because a vegetable has primary life force, it has grown directly from sunlight, air, water and earth. Foods low in vibration or life force such as beef can be seen to hold a secondary or weaker life force.

This is because animals are sustained and survive through vegetation or other animals therefore when we eat them we are 'missing a cycle' in the vital nutrients and life force energy (which we could get by eating the crop directly as opposed to the animal who ate the crop). The pain, suffering and trauma of animals we eat being stored in the cells is also another significant factor in the life force of foods we eat but we won't go into this in detail. Essentially, foods high in vibration are ones which are still in their primary cycle such as the wholefoods, therefore changing your diet to align with this will not only help you feel better, more energized and lighter but will also strengthen your inner chi to be able to protect and ground yourself; which is essential when dealing with any codependent issue or toxic person.

Meditate

Meditation can be used daily to strengthen inner chi as you are literally filling yourself up with space. This strengthens your inner systems and has a range of effects, which ultimately result in your ability to retain your strength and boundaries in addition to your mind being on point. Incorporate the meditation exercises from and set your intention on connecting to your inner chi. This will really help increase both your sense of self and your inner boundaries.

Furthermore, meditation can help you become a better observer of your thoughts and be less reactive to toxic people, as briefly explored earlier. It can help you cultivate patience and be more responsive and

centered, further increasing your ability to leave any harmful or destructive cycles and interactions. Meditation can also increase wisdom and your sense of intuition, so you know when a relationship can be salvaged and when it simply is time to walk away and have that self- love and respect you know you deserve.

Conclusion

I have worked with individuals who experience the ill effects of codependency for certain years and it never neglects to stun me how satisfied these individuals are the point at which they think outside the box and venture past it.

Try not to empower individuals who don't attempt to improve their lives. Try not to put yourself down for not being who they need you to be. Be glad for what your identity is. That is the most important blessing you can ever give anybody on the planet.

There is much bliss to be had after codependence. On the off chance that you truly need to get past it, this book holds every one of the pieces of information. You should simply make the strides that are sketched out in the book and you will slowly discover your way back to wellbeing again and back to a solid perspective where you value yourself and set limits that help other people to regard you. This book was composed with a great deal of feeling since this is a passionate dependent upon me and to the people, I have needed to manage throughout the years who experienced the impacts of codependency. When you figure out how to proceed onward and to set down what are adequate limits, you help everybody – including that individual who may have started to underestimate you.

Once a codependent person is able to understand their disease, they can break the cycle of their impulsive self-betrayal. When a person is in the thick of a codependent relationship, the painful and dysfunctional aspects can make it seem like it is impossible to stop the codependent tendencies. However, when a person is motivated, they can stop the cycle and lead a healthier life.

Some possible steps to breaking the cycle of codependency will actually utilize a great deal of the information provided. Before a person takes the necessary steps to stop the cycle of codependency, they will recognize the signs, symptoms, and past experiences that have led to the codependent tendencies. It is not until after this has been done that the individual can begin to have healthier relationships in the future. It is also true if a person is attempting to stop their codependent tendencies in their current relationship. However, the person suffering from the disease should also take the time to understand whether or not their current partner is enabling the person's codependent behavior because they are a toxic or abusive partner. If that is the case, the codependent person should exit the relationship as soon as possible.

With the practicing of self-care, the codependent person is taking the time to explore themselves instead of just their partner.

The exploration into one's self should focus on the wants and needs of the codependent person as well as their likes, dislikes, and feelings.

If a codependent person does not take the time to explore the necessary steps of learning about one's self and what they need out of their relationships, then they will likely find themselves slipping back into their old habits of helping others and putting other people's.

Lightning Source UK Ltd.
Milton Keynes UK
UKHW022229080621
385174UK00002B/189